T0155127

The Radical Edge

The Radical Edge

Another Personal Lesson in Extreme Leadership

Steve Farber

The Radical Edge: Another Personal Lesson in Extreme Leadership

© 2014-2019 by Extreme Leadership, Inc.

ISBN-13: 9780989300223

For information on distribution rights, royalties, derivative works or licensing opportunities on behalf of this content or work, please contact Mision Boulevard Press and Digital at the address below or via email at info@missionboulevardpress.com.

COMPANIES, ORGANIZATIONS, INSTITUTIONS, AND INDUSTRY PUBLICATIONS: Quantity discounts are available on bulk purchases of this book for reselling, educational purposes, subscription incentives, gifts, sponsorship, or fundraising. Special books or book excerpts can also be created to fit specific needs such as private labeling with your logo on the cover and a message from a VIP printed inside. Contact veronica@missionboulevardpress.com or call 858-513-4184.

Mission Boulevard Press and Digital
1501 India Street, Suite 103-86 San Diego, CA 92101
info@missionboulevardpress.com

This book was printed in the United States of America

Cover design: Joy Stauber
Book interior design: Abbey Gaterud
Skater illustration: Design Solutions
Photo illustration: Lizzie Callen
Photo: Veer

Book set in Warnock Pro

Love All Serve All
—The Hard Rock Café

*There are many people who think they want to
be matadors, only to find themselves in the ring
with two thousand pounds of bull bearing down
on them, and then discover that
what they really wanted was to wear tight pants
and hear the crowd roar.*
—Terry Pearce

CONTENTS

Introduction

In the years since my first book, *The Radical Leap*, was first published, I've heard from countless business people about the importance of LEAP (cultivate Love, generate Energy, inspire Audacity, and provide Proof) in their own endeavors at work. I've met many of these folks and have seen the awesome things they're doing—and attempting to do—to make their colleagues', employees', and customers' lives more meaningful by applying the practices of Extreme Leadership.

And that's unbelievably gratifying, to be sure.

But here's what's really blown my mind: I've also heard from students struggling with who they want to be and what they want to do, graduates nervously embarking on fledgling careers, clergy inspiring their congregations, and teachers tackling the sticky challenges of education. They were not—as we say in business—my "target market"; yet, LEAP has given each of them a good dose of inspiration and a road map to change their lives for the better.

Now that's what gets me out of bed in the morning.

The Radical Edge is also a story—a parable, if you will—about Extreme Leadership. Yes, it's for business people, and, yes, it's for anyone else, too. Wherever you are in your life, and whatever position you may hold (or aspire to hold) at work, I believe the principles in these pages will stoke your fires, amp your volume, and help you change your world—whatever that world may be.

The characters you are about to meet represent people (or

combinations of people) who've inspired me over the years. The same goes for the places and events. In other words, I've jumbled the made–up stuff with the "real" to the point that I'm not even sure where the facts end and the fiction begins. But that's what made writing it so much fun.

The important thing, though, is that the ideas, principles, and actions are as real as it gets. You're about to take a journey into the elements of personal and professional transformation. May it bring you higher levels of business success, deepened personal clarity, and a greater ability to shape your world.

May it bring you to The Radical Edge.

The Radical Edge

Another Personal Lesson in Extreme Leadership

Prologue

I was stuck deep in the wilds of Michigan, in the middle of winter, on the back end of a raging snowstorm that had left the countryside covered in—what do poets like to call it?—"a downy soft blanket of white." That sounds much nicer than "a blinding, frozen wasteland," which is a much more accurate image. I wasn't exactly stranded out on the tundra, however, I was holed up in a toasty conference room inside a quaint but efficient bed and breakfast built for the burgeoning corporate off-site market. Moreover, I wasn't alone because I was facilitating an executive retreat for, and I mean this in the nicest way, a roomful of middle-aged, white guys named "Jim."

Blatant gender and ethnic homogeneity aside, this was a group of very intelligent, dependable, and steadfast mid- to senior-level managers of a large Cedar Rapids–based manufacturing company, and I was an experienced and newly re-energized leadership consultant on a mission. The group was thrashing around trying to come to terms with a question that I had just dropped on them like a sack of salt on the roadway. It wasn't the kind of question that they teach in facilitator school—such as, for example, "Who would like to volunteer to jump out of a tree?"—but a question that demanded the group look at their role and their company's role from an entirely different perspective. A question that required a very deep level of thought and reflection as well as a steroidal dose of intellectual and moral courage, and that reflected my new perspective on the nature of meaningful life and work in the twenty-first century:

"How are we going to change the world?"

Apparently, it was a question that invited the inner cynic frothing with spittle and ablaze with venom to emerge, as well.

"Are you kidding me? What kind of question is that?" raged Jim.

"Ummm, a really important one?" I offered.

"How is that supposed to help me with my ridiculous workload, Steve? I mean, c'mon."

"Look," said another Jim. "I think it's a good question. I think we should be willing to consider it at least. It'll make for a good discussion, anyway." Several Jims nodded in support.

"Hold on," said Cynical Jim. "I don't think this is just about having a discussion." He looked at me. "I'm assuming that you don't want us to just talk about how we're going to change the world, you want us to do it. Am I right?"

"Yeah. That's about right."

"One question for you, then, Steve."

"Okay."

"Assuming that we spend the time on this instead of the other really important questions that we need to address at this meeting, and assuming that we actually come up with an answer—"

"Good assumptions," I encouraged.

"Okay, then here's the question I'll want answered. What, exactly, does a person like me need to do to make it all happen?"

"You mean what do you personally have to do to change the world?"

"As long as we're asking the deep questions, yeah."

"And another thing," said another Jim. "We do have a business to run here. Are we just supposed to forget about that while we're out changing the world?"

"Yeah," said yet another, "not to mention having something resembling a personal life in our spare time."

I paused. I looked out the window. I looked back at Jim. I opened my mouth. I closed it again. These were damned good questions.

I wished I had the answers.

A WUP Upside the Head

1.

I live in the Mission Beach area of San Diego, California. It's a bit different from Michigan, especially in the wintertime, and I was desperately trying to get back there after my conference with the Jims. There are no direct flights from Cedar Rapids to San Diego International Airport, unless you had enough cake to hire your own personal jet, which, of course, I didn't. I was prowling the sleek metal and glass halls of O'Hare and killing time as I waited for my connection, which was delayed for an unspecified amount of time. I had ignored the gate agent's admonishment to "remain comfortably seated in the boarding area" in case the weather gods suddenly changed their game plan. The airline was having enough trouble negotiating their pilot contracts let alone getting cooperation from the supreme powers that be, so I bugged out to wander the concourse and pump a little blood into my travel weary brain cells.

I had a lot to think about. The meeting had gone okay, I guess. They had all left thinking much bigger thoughts than what they'd come in with, and I felt really good about that. A shift in perspective is no small thing, to be sure, but I was feeling the dull ache of regret—or was it discontent?—that I used to get after teaching the canned, scripted workshops that were the staples of my earlier days in the leadership development business. Don't get me wrong, I loved the idea of changing the world as the core business and leadership proposition, but I still found myself doubting my ability to actually get it done. I didn't want people to mention the names of Don Quixote and Steve Farber in the same breath. Tilting unabashedly at windmills is one thing; slaying dragons is a whole 'nother smoke.

I turned a corner and found myself face-to-face with a large and very odd billboard advertisement. It was a picture of a blue Oxford button-down shirt with a red power necktie, and it would have been the classic image of clean, conservative business, if not for one bizarre detail: the tie was on fire. Accompanying it was a big, bold headline that read, "Burn Your Boss" and a tagline at the bottom that said, "Report the use of unlicensed software." This was, essentially, an invitation—no, a challenge—for a person to spy on and rat out their management, and it was punctuated with an 800-number hotline for people to *call right now* and strike the sparkling, gratifying match of revenge.

Now I have as much respect for intellectual property rights as the next guy. Probably more. I'm not a fan of pirating or plagiarism. I sided with Metallica over the early Napster debates and will gladly pop for a buck a song to download to my iPod as opposed to trolling the web for free sources. Software's in the same category, especially on an enterprise level. However, "Burn Your Boss?" Have things really gotten that bad? Did these people honestly expect to tap into some unexpressed reservoir of rage trembling under the surface of other business travelers like myself? More importantly, was this ad working? There was one way to find out. I called the number.

I was hoping to get a live person on the line so I could simply ask the question. What I got, though, was a recorded message saying something about their organization and their office hours followed by an invitation to leave your information—about that evil boss, I assumed—after the tone. As to the question of whether their ad was working, I got my answer right away. Before I could say anything, their machine spoke to me. It said, "You cannot leave a message because the mailbox is full."

2.

I shoveled the gobs of mail from my box, punched in the security code on the front door, and climbed the two flights of stairs to my apartment overlooking Mission Bay. It was always strange to return home to an empty perch and see how much dust had managed to accumulate on the kitchen counters in just one week. The sea air mixed with fine sand always found its way in with or without the security code.

Like scratching for gems in a litter box, I sifted through the mail—junk, bills, a belated birthday card from my dentist, a check from a recent client project—and threw the whole pile on the round oak kitchen table. There was one item that looked a bit more personal, so I picked it up for closer inspection. I tore open the envelope to find a delicate, handcrafted note card from my friend, Janice, who was a grand high muckity-muck at a local bio-tech company. Janice and I were old friends, and I had recently helped her out of a sticky career jam. The handwritten words inside the card offered a friendly thinking of you kind of sentiment followed by a postscript reading,

> *I've given your name to my friend, Rich Delacroix,*
> *CEO of Independence Lending Group. He may be*
> *calling you for a coaching engagement. He's a nice*
> *man. Please don't hurt him.*

She followed it with one of those endearing little emoticons to indicate that she was smiling about that last part.

I rooted around in my empty kitchen but no amount of persistence was going to uncover anything resembling food. As I headed back out the door for a Jack in the Box run, my cell jangled a funky electronic tune.

"Steve Farber?" inquired the voice on the other end of the line. "This is Rich Delacroix. Janice gave me your number. I know this is short notice, but do you, by chance, have time for a quick visit to my office?"

Here in the twenty-first century, the archetypal call to action mostly comes via the digital phone. Jack, I thought wistfully, would have to wait in his box a little bit longer.

Independence Lending Group, Inc.'s (ILGI) snappy commercials promising the best mortgage rates and fastest service on the planet were plastered all over the television and radio airwaves. Maybe they were true; all I knew was that the company had grown like gangbusters during the nuclear boom in the real estate market and the feverish refi activity fueled by subterranean interest rates. I'm usually not impressed by people who make fortunes in bull markets, even though, come to think of it, I never have, but this was one of the few mortgage companies that also managed to survive the subsequent economic melt-down. And that was noteworthy.

ILGI's corporate offices were in La Jolla's University Town Center (UTC) neighborhood. UTC is a cement and glass amalgam of apartments, office buildings, malls, restaurants, and a Mormon temple that keeps an impressive and watchful eye over the endless traffic on Interstate 5. I parked my Mustang in the visitor's parking structure and took the elevator up to the eighteenth floor. The receptionist announced my name into the phone, and before I had a chance to settle into a plush leather chair, Rich Delacroix came bounding through the door on the far end of the waiting area. He was young—mid thirties, I guessed—tan, fit, blond, energetic and, although his attire was casual, exceedingly well dressed.

Despite all that, I liked him immediately.

He gripped my hand with an unsurprising firmness and ushered me into his corner office with a view of the Mormon temple that overlooks the endless traffic on Interstate 5. I got lost for a moment in the symbolic possibilities.

"Steve," he said. "Thanks so much for taking the time to come over. I know you're a busy man with a lot on your plate. So let's get down to it, okay?"

He walked me over to a small conference area in the corner of his corner office, and this time I did sink down into a beautiful, rich, brown leather chair.

"Happy to help if I can, Rich," I said. "What is it that you need?"

"Me, personally? Nothing." I raised my eyebrows, and he hesitated for a moment. "I don't mean it to sound that way, I'm not perfect…that's not what I mean. But I have a very weak link in my management team, and he's the one that really needs help—or that I need help with."

It was really rather endearing to see this supremely self-possessed individual squirm as if he had a tapeworm.

This was not a dude who was used to asking anyone for help, let alone a virtual stranger.

"Okay, lay it on me," I said taking out my yellow legal pad. "Give me the whole story."

3.

Closer, dealmaker, phone demon, top producer, Cameron Summerfield is a sales god. He came to work at ILGI fresh out of state college where he'd graduated unceremoniously with a liberal arts degree. Armed with a diploma on the wall and the money bug up his butt, he finagled an interview at the exploding mortgage company and, of course, nailed it. He raced through training and attacked the phone with the enthusiasm and compassion of a taunted pit bull, setting a record for new loans in a single month in the first month of his career. His third month on the phone yielded a commission check of eighty thousand dollars. That's not a misprint, and it was no fluke. Cam was golden week in and week out. He bought a loft in downtown San Diego, a Blaupunkt sound system, and a Porsche Carrera. He was twenty-six years old.

Now he was the youngest senior vice president in the history of the company. His promotion, it was beginning to seem, being Rich Delacroix's big mistake. The problem, apparently, was really pretty simple: the salespeople, who all ultimately reported to Cam, hated his guts with a steaming passion. Turnover, which was already high in the mortgage industry, was through the roof, and ILGI's best sales talent was bailing at an alarming rate.

"Why? What's he doing that's so despicable?"

"Look," Rich said. "Don't misunderstand, I happen to like Cam very much, and there's no doubt that he's an extraordinary salesman, but leadership doesn't come as naturally to him as closing deals. I want him to make this work, but he's flat-out brutal with the sales team. I'm a believer in incentives and disincentives, too; I like a little friendly competition among the team. But he takes it all too far."

"I'm going to need you to be more specific, Rich. I could interpret that in all kinds of ways. I mean, brutal is a pretty strong word. He's not, like, jamming wood splints into the soles of people's feet, right? So what does Cam's brutality look like?"

"I'm not going to tell you that right now."

"Really? Why?"

Rich pointed over my shoulder and I looked back as the door swung slowly open. "Okay to come in?" called a voice from the hallway.

"Give us a few more minutes, Cam. Be right with you." The door shut with a quiet click.

"Oh. So you just want me to dive right in, huh?" I paused for a second before continuing. "Tell you what, Rich. I don't really know if I can help or not, but I'll make you a deal. Starting tomorrow morning let me hang out with Cam for a day or so, get to know him a bit. If we hit it off you can start paying me. If we don't get along, we'll part ways and I won't send you a bill."

"Sorry," he replied. "I'm a little confused. You want to hang out with him? What does that have to do with coaching?"

"Do me a favor," I said. "Go over to your computer and Google executive coach." He remained seated, staring at me. "C'mon. Humor me."

Rich walked over to his desk, typed the words on his keyboard, and hit return.

"How many hits?" I asked.

He raised his eyebrows. "3,520,000."

"Add another seven hundred thousand or so for leadership coach and 130 grand for management coach and you get the picture, right? Listen, Rich, there are a lot of great coaches out there and some very fine coaching associations and curricula available to those who want to learn how to coach. But anyone can hang out a shingle on the Web and spend an hour a week on the phone with a client, and any one of them would be more than happy to work with Cam."

"Okay..."

"I won't, though, unless..."

"Unless what?" Rich interrupted.

I shrugged. "Unless I like him."

4.

I was flying once from New York to San Francisco after conducting a workshop in which I'd talked nonstop for two straight days. Now I'm not saying it was two days of sparkling verbal gems, mind you, but talk takes energy and mine was gone. Cashing in my first-class upgrades and relaxing in total, blissful silence with a good novel was what I desired the most. Golden ticket in hand, I stood in the boarding line and watched as they loaded up the families traveling with small children contingent. Inching toward the Jetway, a young woman dragged her squirming little boy by the hand. He wailed and howled at the top of his lungs as though she were tearing off his little digits one by one.

Having traveled with my own kids when they were little, I know how stressful a fussy child can be for the parent. Just as I was thinking how difficult this flight was going to be for the young mom, this guy standing in front of me yelled, "*I knew it! I knew it!* I heard that kid screaming in the terminal and I said, 'that kid's gonna be on my flight!' *I knew it.* It never fails!"

What a jerk, I remember thinking. That poor woman was feeling bad enough already. She needed this jerk's vociferous commentary as much as she needed a rabid hyena strapped to her leg.

A few minutes later I walked on the plane and to my horror I realized who my seatmate was: The Jerk. I felt like screaming *I knew it! Every time there's a jerk on the plane they end up next to me!* But I didn't. Instead, I sat down, buckled up, pulled out my book, and locked my eyes on the pages. I sent out megatons of don't talk to me vibes and felt confident there was no way he would dare to reach through my pulsating, death star force field. He couldn't possibly have the gall to...

"Hey! Waddaya reading? Oh! I read that book! I've read everything by that guy! Do you live in Frisco or are you going there to work? Man, am I glad I'm not sitting next to that *kid*. Did you hear that kid screamin'? Hey! Waddaya wanna drink?" He waved a hand in the air. "Waitress! They hate that, har-har-har! We are ready to start *drinkin'*!"

This situation is what's known in behavioral psychology circles as a lost cause, so I closed my book, accepted the drink, resigned myself to several hours of pressurized cabin torture, and threw myself at the mercy of the verbose and soon to be plastered Jerk Man. Funny thing is, I had a great time.

Sure, Jerk Man was a bit over the top. He was too loud, and, yeah, he had the emotional intelligence of a bottlenose fly, and I don't mean that in a judgmental way, but he was interesting, eccentric, and a gifted raconteur. In short, by the time we landed in San Francisco, I was glad I'd met him.

"Pretty funny," said Rich. "I assume you're telling me this for a reason?"

"Yeah. Of course. Let me ask you a question with a ridiculously obvious answer. Why was Jerk Man talking to me?"

"What do you mean?"

"I mean why was he talking to me and not the guy sitting back in 10C?"

Rich furrowed his eyebrows. "Ummm...because he was sitting next to you?"

"Right. I was strapped in next to him and not going anywhere for several hours. We talked and got to know each other for one simple, profoundly obvious reason: I was there."

"Okay," mumbled Rich, still not seeing my point.

"Proximity. Physical nearness. Face-to-face and shoulder-to-shoulder, Rich. That's the only way to really connect with another human being because that's the only way we really get to know each other."

"And that's why you want to hang out with Cam."

"And that's why I want to hang out with Cam."

"Okay, I get it, Steve. One question, though: after hanging out with Cam, talking with him, getting to know him, what if you don't like him? Does that really mean that you won't work with him?"

"I wouldn't worry about that."

"Why?"

I grinned. "Because I like everybody."

5.

Rich punched a button on his phone and a few minutes later Cam threw the door open and sauntered into the office. He looked like—how can I say this nicely—a cocky *GQ* wannabe. He wore tasseled loafers, wool pants with razor-sharp pleats, a silk shirt, and enough hair products to slick a porcupine. He may as well have been wearing a sign saying, *I make money.* I really do try to resist snap judgments, but my first thought, I have to admit, was *Danger, Will Robinson!* I stood up and shook his hand as Rich made the introductions.

"So," said Cam as he gave me the once-over, "I understand you're going to give me some of the latest, cutting-edge sales techniques. I'm all ears for anything that'll keep me on top of my game, dude."

I looked at Rich. "Sales techniques?"

He flushed. "Well, Cam, that's not exactly what I had in mind by inviting Steve to work with you."

Cam stiffened as if someone had just stuck a live wire down his Armanis. "What do you mean?" The question caught in his throat. "What's goin' on here?"

"I'm more of a leadership coach, Cam. Extreme Leadership," I said in a Bond, James Bond sort of way. "Rich has asked me to help you get a handle on leading your sales team."

"Why?" he asked, shooting a look at Rich.

"Look, Cam," Rich began. "It couldn't hurt for you to expand your skills in that area. We all know that you're the man when it comes to selling. No one's going to argue that point. But... you've got to get your leadership act together if you're going to be a part of this company's future. Don't act as if this is a total surprise. It's not like we haven't talked about this before, right?"

Now it was Cam's turn to flush. I watched the redness rise from his neck to his ears to the top of his forehead. *Thar she blows!* I thought. Then as quickly as his skin had erupted, the color dissipated and he regained his composure.

"Okay, sure, fine. Whatever," he huffed. "When do we start?"

"Tomorrow morning," I said.

"And what do we do first?"

"We have breakfast."

6.

The morning was gray and overcast; the kind of day that gives June Gloom its name. This was December, however, and the Mission Beach coastline was doing that water and sand thing without the slightest inclination or care about what my day was going to be like. I don't know why I love gray beach days. Maybe it's because they make me look differently at the pounding waves and squawking seagulls. The birds and the waves don't care if the sun's out or not. That's not a bad attitude for a human to adopt.

Just before the north end of Mission Beach turns into Pacific Beach, Mission Café abuts the boardwalk. You can get a cup of coffee and a muffin and sit right outside where the action is. Cam and I found a spot at a table behind the short retaining wall that separated the porch from the boardwalk. I took in a full, deep breath of sea air. Man, what could be better? My morning coffee, steaming and potent; the Pacific, rolling and churning; the beach walkers, strolling and talking, all of it reminding me— not that I needed it— of how much I loved this place. The air smelled of suntan lotion, which told me that despite the cloud cover, the early morning crowd was characteristically optimistic.

I'm always amazed by the variety of earnest morning walkers: college kids clipping along in their baseball caps, cargo shorts, and tight-laced Adidas, older folks glad still to be walking at all, skaters on their boards, and bikers riding backwards on their handlebars. It's quite a parade— not the kind that would have inspired John Philip Sousa, but I never really cared for his music anyway.

All this I kept to myself. Cam, however, was more external with his thoughts than I was. I slowly realized that he was spewing forth an endless stream of color commentary on the overweight, over-thin, over-plasticized, over—or under—whatever of every person passing by. He didn't realize it, but he was pushing my buttons as rapidly and aggressively as a rat beeping a scientist for food. It didn't sound like anger so much as condescension, arrogance, and an overall *these people suck* perspective on the scene.

"Jeez! Look at *that* guy. Can you believe him? He looks like a dog I used to own. Get a load of that hair. What a fleabag!" He gave me a conspiratorial nudge on the arm. "What sewer did he sleep in last night?"

The current object of Cam's attention was, indeed, a little scruffy looking, I suppose. He was tall and wiry, and his too-tan arms poked out from the cutoff sleeves of a blue tie-dyed

T-shirt. Green khaki cargo shorts and Reef flip-flops completed what was a fairly run-of-the-mill beach ensemble. However, it was his amazing hair that set him apart from the rest of the crowd: prolific red dreadlocks fell down from the top of his head, and, beginning just beneath a wide, prominent nose that held up round, lemon yellow sunglasses, a giant, red mustache and beard stuck out in all directions at once. As if on cue, the sewer dog in question launched himself over the retaining wall, scooped up a chair, and swung it over to our table. He sat down next to Cam and across from me as though we'd been expecting him all along. Truth was I had. If our visitor's unruly, red beard really had been casting off fleas, Cam's mouth would have caught them all.

"Here's the funny thing, Cam," I said, enjoying his shock. "This fleabag here is a friend of mine, and, it just so happens, he's our breakfast date." I could feel my smile broadening as I watched Cam digest this bit of news.

Smitty grinned at Cam and then bear slapped me on the back like he always did. "Farberoni, my man, it's a great day to be alive and kickin', especially considering the alternative." Smitty's laugh is infectious. It starts somewhere deep down in his body and seems to ripple all the way to the ends of each red hair—and that's a lot of rippling. Cam, however, looked as if he was afraid of other infectious things.

"Smitty, I'd like you to meet Cam; Cam, my friend Smitty here is one of the wisest people I've ever met, and I'm not embarrassed to say so."

"And I ain't embarrassed to hear you say it. It's a pleasure, Mr. Cam," Smitty said, extending his tan, weathered hand. Cam shook it without much exuberance, but Smitty wouldn't let go.

He gripped Cam's hand as if he was trying to squeeze a marble out of a fish. "Dang, son! You look a lot peppier than you are." Smitty leaned in close to Cam and whispered, "You been drinkin' your milk?"

Cam's face reddened and he squeezed back.

"Don't get angry now, son," said Smitty. "I'm just messin' with ya. Now why don't you order me a coffee, here, Farberama. And get this boy a glass of moo juice. I'll be right back. The lizard's barkin', if you know what I mean." He jumped up and ran off to find the public terrarium, if I knew what he meant.

"What the hell was *that* all about?" hissed Cam. "Are you really expecting me to waste my time like this? I thought you were supposed to be coaching me." He said *coaching* like he was trying to eject something nasty from the back of his throat.

I gazed out at the water and calmly replied. "Listen, Cam. Give Smitty a chance; you may be surprised what you can learn from him. Appearances aren't always what they seem, right?"

"Wait a minute," he said in amazement. "I just thought that he was your friend. Are you trying to tell me that he's here to help me? This is a joke, right?" He waited for me to answer. "Right?"

Smitty returned much faster than I'd thought possible, but there he was parking himself next to Cam and cozying in nice and close.

Cam leaned back in his chair. "What is this?" he said looking over at Smitty. "*A Christmas Carol*? When do I meet the ghosts of breakfasts past and future?"

Well, well! Cam has a sense of humor. I had to admit I was impressed by his joke, despite the spiteful tone.

"Something bothering you, son?" said Smitty. "Is there something you wanna say to me?"

"Yeah."

"Well go on, then."

"Stop calling me son."

"Sorry, Buck. I don't mean nothin' by it. Just a Texas habit. So tell me a little about yourself."

"Like what?" Cam said with a sniff.

"Well, for starters: where'd you go to school?"

"San Diego State. Graduated with a degree in Sorority Relations and I was immediately brought into ILGI where I decided pretty damn quickly to take no prisoners. Four years later, I'm twenty-six, I'm senior vice president of a mortgage company with over one thousand people on the payroll, and it's up to me to make sure we're closing deals and writing loans. And I've got my boys and girls whipped into shape." He popped his sleeve over the enormous watch on his wrist.

"All right, then. You like to read? Read any management stuff?" Smitty asked, as he started mixing half a dozen packets of sugar into his coffee.

Cam raised his eyebrows at the empty sugar packets collecting one by one on the table. "I don't have time to read books that tell me what I already know. Not to sound arrogant or anything but I've got, like, instinct or something. You can't teach that. I can smell a deal. All I need is that feeling, and…BAM…another client for the company and money in my pocket. And, by the way, it's not chump change I'm talking about."

"Well, Buck, I'll bet you just about got it all, then—the Porsche, the kick-ass apartment in the city, designer clothes, martinis at The Bitter End, steaks at Donovan's, and more bling for your many young ladies then they could wear in a year. That about right?"

"That's about right, *Buck*." Cam said proudly looking my way. "Can we go now? I've got a sales team to run."

"Now hold on a minute, there, Buck!" hollered Smitty. Several people at other tables looked our way to see what the fuss was about, and Smitty instinctively lowered the volume on his Texas boombox voice.

"Just relax," he said quieter. "You're getting the wrong idea. You're thinkin' that I'm some kinda money's-the-root-of-all-evil kinda guy. That I'm gonna tell you that the pursuit of material things is shameful. And that you're a shallow, shallow little boy."

Cam shrugged indifferently. "I don't really care what you think of me, to tell you the truth. But, yeah, that's what it sounds like, and I don't need a lecture in ethics. There's nothing wrong with the way I live, so butt out."

This was not going quite as well as I'd hoped.

"Smitty," I interrupted. "Fair's fair. Since you're giving Cam the third degree, why don't you tell him a bit about your background?"

"You betcha. Happy to oblige." He turned to Cam. "Ever hear of a little company called Maritime?"

"Maritime and Son? Sure, who hasn't?"

"I was CIO."

7.

Cam just about swallowed his tongue. "You were the chief information officer of Maritime and Son?" he asked incredulously.

"No, sir, I was not."

"But you just said..."

"I said CIO, not chief information officer. Really, Buck, do I look like the type?" And here came the rippling, deep laughter that I loved so much. "I was the clear insight officer, is what I was. Yeah, yeah, I know it sounds contrived, but William Maritime himself gave me the title, Buck, and that was back before those kinds of titles were trendy. So I wasn't about to argue, and you wouldn't have neither."

The name of William Maritime got Cam's attention, and for good reason. Maritime, known as Pops to his friends, was a business legend and a builder of fortunes. I was fortunate enough to have connected with him personally just before he passed away. In retrospect, my brief meeting with Pops had been the most valuable afternoon of my life.

"My job, Buck, was to keep the company awake, alive, and alert to the world outside the walls of the Maritime empire. 'The only way to change the world is to be fully in it, my young friend,' is what Pops said to me when I first joined on as an intern in my last summer as a graduate student. So, I tried to live fully in the world—to watch, stay awake, pay attention, and try to extract meaning and significance from everything I saw. Then I'd go back to the company and share what I'd learned. I became what you might call the corporate anthropologist, the applied futurist. Once upon a time, I explained to Farber here that I'm a sign reader. I take the lay of the land and all its inhabitants runnin' around it, and then try and see things, with as much clarity as I can muster, from their perspective. That's how you keep learnin' and that's how you get and keep a radical edge in your business and in your life overall."

Cam raised an eyebrow. "And they paid you for that?"

"Mucho dinero, Buck. And worth every shekel, if I do say so m'self. Which I do."

"Let me get this straight," he said with not a little bit of skepticism. "You're telling me that Mr. Maritime paid you a small fortune to what? Observe things?"

Smitty winked at me from behind his yellow shades. "I never said small."

"Not that it really matters, Cam," I said. "But Smitty's done all right for himself. Now do yourself a favor and just listen to him for a minute, will you, please?" I could feel the stiletto heels of impatience tap-dancing on the back of my neck.

"All right, then!" crowed Smitty as he clapped his hands together. "Let's start with the basics. First of all, you have to do what you can to learn from the great ones. Make sense?"

Cam nodded. "To tell you the truth, back when I first started working at ILGI, I listened to a ton of sales training audios—Hopkins, Waitley, Gitomer, guys like that."

"Excellenté. Courses can help, but did you know that Farber here is one of the great ones?"

Cam looked at me and I looked at Smitty. I could feel my face reddening. "Well, that's nice of you to say, Smitty, but I'm not that special. I'm just trying to..."

"Hush up," he said, "and let me finish."

I sat quietly in the glow of the unexpected and deeply satisfying compliment.

Smitty pointed out toward the beach. "See that tourist with the high-top sneakers? Also one of the great ones. The lady with the mouthful of cheese Danish at the table over there? A great one if ever there was one." He jabbed his finger through the air at every person walking by on the boardwalk. "Great, great, great, great."

And I swear he'd still be sitting there great-ing away if Cam hadn't reached out and snatched Smitty's finger in his hand.

"Okay, I get what you're saying. *We're all great ones,*" Cam oozed in a cynical, syrupy voice.

"Yeah, I knew that," I mumbled.

"This ain't no platitude, boys." I noticed that Smitty had made me a part of his audience. "If you assume that you can learn from anyone—if you assume that you must learn from *everyone*—then everyone becomes a great teacher for you. Even if someone's a slime sucking scumbag of a leech, they qualify for greatness if you can learn something from them."

"Okay then," said Cam. "I'm a kick-ass twenty-six-year-old sales executive. Let's see what you can learn from me."

That got my goat right in the sweets. "Let's get clear on the concept, Cam," I growled through my teeth. "I'd like you to see what you can learn from Smitty, not the other way around."

"Bad Farber!" Smitty admonished in a dog trainer tone. "He's got a good point. No doubt that we all have much to learn from you, Buck, and I'd love to hear your whole story sometime in the very near future."

"It's Cam."

"For right now, though, Cam, I got something that'll help both you and Mr. Farberacious here to become CIOs yourselves."

"Sounds cool to me," I said. I always found Smitty's perspective refreshing and surprising. To him, good advice was everywhere; you just had to be alert enough to notice and care enough to ask yourself the right questions about the nature of the world and its inhabitants. A sudden smacking pain on my right ear jolted me back to attention. "Yow! Jeez, Smitty, what the hell'd you do that for?" I yelped, palming my ear. He had slapped me on the side of the head with a small spiral-bound notebook, which now lay innocently on the table in front of me.

Smitty laughed, which really ticked me off. "Aw, c'mon now, Stevie. That was just a friendly little WUP upside your head. We all need that from time to time, don't we?"

"Yeah, well, I read *A Whack on the Side of the Head* a long time ago, Smitty." I said fondling my ear, more from shock than from pain. "But I don't think it was supposed to be taken literally."

"Whack, wup, smack, all the same idea. We gotta keep ourselves from falling asleep at the wheel. Sometimes literally, but, you're right-o, Farbo, I was just makin' a point in my own impish but endearing sort of way." He picked up the little notebook—aka weapon—and dangled it in front of Cam and me. "This ain't a notebook; it's a WUP."

"A WUP," I repeated. Cam let out a deep sigh and looked at his watch.

"Yup, a WUP. Stands for Wake-Up Pad, and it's the most important little life shifter that you're ever gonna find, if you use it right. Matter of fact, if you don't use it right it is just another notebook. But if you do," he leaned close to Cam, "it'll bring you more money than you have ever made, my young Rock-a-fella."

"Explain," said Cam with slightly more enthusiasm than he'd shown so far, which wasn't saying much.

"In a minute," he said and then looked my way. "And you, Farbio, are takin' up the call to change the world for the better, eh?"

"Trying to."

"Good! But you know what?" He waggled his WUP. "You ain't gonna get nowhere without the wisdom contained in this little puppy right here."

"Smitty. C'mon," I said, awakening the skeptic within. "I don't see what difference a notebook is..."

"It's a WUP!" he boomed. "*A Wake-Up Pad.* Here, take it." He shoved it at me. "Open'er up and look at what's inside."

Okay, I mused, *there's got to be something really extraordinary in this thing.* Starting to feel a little jolt of anticipation, I slowly turned the card stock cover to reveal the first page of Smitty's WUP. It was extraordinary.

Extraordinarily blank.

8.

While I was staring, incredulous, at that blank sheet of paper, Rich Delacroix had just started a senior management meeting in the oak paneled conference room at the national headquarters of Independence Lending Group, Inc. The topic at hand, I would later find out, was the uncertain future of one Cam Summerfield, SVP of sales.

"Folks," said Rich, "I want your help with the impending crisis on the sales team. If things don't change soon, we're going to lose a lot of good people and it's going to be a real bitch to hit the numbers we need for the next expansion phase."

"Isn't that what we pay Cam for?" asked Sharon Washington, SVP of underwriting. "Shouldn't he be here for this discussion?"

"Yes, he should," said Rich, "except for one small thing." He raised his eyebrows and exhaled a sigh ripe with the unspoken but obvious reality.

"Cam is the problem." Sharon completed the thought for him.

"Do we have anyone else ready to step in for Cam?" A fidgety, uncomfortable silence permeated the room as the implications of Rich's question hit home.

"Are you going to fire him?"

"Not necessarily. He's got one last chance to start getting his leadership act together."

"How long are we giving him to show some improvement?"

"One day."

"Generous," Sharon oozed. "What if," she continued sarcastically, "he doesn't get hit by lightning, or his lobotomy doesn't take? Are you going to fire him?"

"No," Rich replied. "Worse. I'm going to demote him."

9.

"Let me see that." Cam snatched the notebook—sorry, *WUP*—away from me, looked at it, and slapped it back down on the table. "Listen," he demanded, "very, very carefully: *I...don't... have...time...for...this.* I'm going back to work," he said to me, "and I'm telling Rich that this didn't work out. Smitty, it's been a real treat, but I'm outie." He pushed his chair back and stood up.

Smitty rose with him, put his hands on Cam's shoulders, and gently pushed him back into his seat.

"Relax, dude," he said in a surprisingly calm voice. "Just hear me out for a minute. I'm gonna tell you how to use this thing, and then you decide if you're innie or outie." It wasn't a request, and he didn't give Cam a chance to protest.

"Number one," Smitty began as he picked up the WUP, "carry this with you at all times. Now a Wake-Up Pad doesn't have to be paper. You could use your iPad, laptop, or a voice recorder on your cell, but just to get the practice down, start with this little book until it becomes like another appendage like your hand or your—well, let's just say your hand.

"Go on," he pushed a pen into Cam's hand. "Write that down: carry at all times." His eyes bored into Cam until he complied.

"Number two." He waited until Cam wrote the number on the pad. "Scan, just like you were a computer scanner. Your scanner just copies; it doesn't comment, it doesn't offer an opinion, it doesn't tell you you're stupid for wasting your time on that photo of the girl you met while y'all were dancin' on the bar at Jimmy Love's. Just scan your environment and record what you see. Scan the bestseller lists and notice what people are reading; scan the magazine racks and pick up publications that don't interest you like, I dunno, *The Tattoo Review* or *Graffiti Today*; scan the weekly TV show rankings; scan the headlines of your online newsfeeds and actual print-and-ink newspapers from twenty different cities; scan what's trending on Twitter; scan the room that you're sitting in; scan the crowd as you're toolin' down the street during your lunch break. Then, every so often, write down what you're seeing in your WUP. Write down your observations of subcultures that are entirely alien to you and trends in the tastes of the popular culture. Capture little ideas, snapshots of natural, political, and social phenomena. Scan, scan, scan. Look at everything going on around you and write your observations in the pad."

"And then what?" Cam asked. "What's the point?" Smitty held up a finger.

"I'm coming to that, but at first all you're doing is scanning the world and writing down what you see without comment or judgment."

I thought about Cam's earlier scathing commentary on the

beach population. "What do you mean by no judgment?" I asked, trying to lead Smitty in a direction that I thought Cam needed to be taken.

"I mean," he said looking right at Cam. "That I ain't no flea-infested guttersnipe, am I, Buck?"

"I'll give you that." Cam conceded. "My first impression of you was wrong."

"Well, now, ain't you the big man for admittin' it? And that's the point, my repentant friend. Observe but don't judge. You might have written a description of me in your WUP, but you'd have left out the arrogant, holier-than-thou attitude. You with me?"

"Yeah," muttered Cam, letting the insult pass like gas in the breeze.

"All right, then. Let's move on to number three."

10.

"Tell me the truth now, Cammie Boy. Have you ever listened in on another person's conversation? Let's say you're standing in line at Starbucks, minding your own business, and there's a couple behind you in line having a little tiff about something or other; his mother, her aerobics instructor, something like that. Tell me that you're not going to listen in."

Cam shrugged. "Yeah, I am."

"Good! Of course you would. Everyone would! You know why? We're interested in the drama of humanity, especially dramas we're not supposed to know anything about. We love those little windows into others' lives. So, I say this: eavesdrop away!

We do it anyway, so why not make it a habit and a practice, and listen in with conscious intent?"

"Say what?" I chirped.

"Oh relax, Farberoosky. I'm not talking about buggin' peoples' offices or anything like that. This is nothin' more than paying attention to what other people are talkin' about. Hell, listening to talk radio is a form of eavesdropping, ain't it? Tune in to both right and left-wing shows and you'll pretty much be listening in on an entire national conversation. *Scan* and *eavesdrop* are basically just lookin' and listenin'. Consider yourself both a scanner and a microphone. Again, you're not making any judgments on what you're seeing or hearing, just collectin' the data that's coming to you.

"Okay, now, the next thing you do is..." Smitty paused and looked at Cam until he got the nonverbal message, picked up his pen, and wrote a nice, clean number four in his evolving WUP. "*Ponder*. After collecting your observations for a while you stop, read it over, and give it some reflection. What are the implications of this? What can I learn from that? Why are so many people doing X, and what might that mean for all of us?

"For example, why are so many people watching reality TV? And why doesn't anyone seem to notice that the phrase reality TV is the ultimate oxymoron? Or maybe one day you were royally ticked off because you were tryin' to do some work on your vacation, but you couldn't get your laptop to connect. So, you had jotted down a note in your WUP that said something like I can't find a flippin' Wi-Fi connection when I really need one. So now you ask the question, what are the implications of anytime, anywhere broadband Internet connections and what's that gonna mean for the way we should sell mortgages in the near future? Now, you don't just ask the questions, you think about the answers. We don't give ourselves nearly enough time to reflect. We think we don't have time. But I'm telling you, if all you're doin' is reacting to things rather than giving yourself the time to ponder, you're gonna be left in the dust without any new ideas. And you certainly won't be leadin' the pack, right, Buck?

"So you see what's starting to happen here, boys?" Smitty was making sure that Cam wasn't the only one hearing the message. "You're observing, processing, interpreting, massaging, and playing with your experience of the human drama—or comedy, more likely—and encouraging your brain to look for new, clear insights which will lead, eventually, to new ways of doing things in your business and in your life."

Cam was actually nodding his head. "It's a brainstorming tool," he said.

"Yeah, think of it that way at first, if you want. Whatever it takes to get you to do it is just fine with me," Smitty chortled and winked at me.

I winked back, but I didn't know why.

11.

"Now, this next step is where the magic happens," Smitty rolled on. "This is what makes the mondo difference, and it's the one thing that note takers since the days of tablets and chisels have rarely even thought about. So write down and underline number five: *Talk about it.*"

"With who?" asked Cam.

"Yeah," I added, finding myself in Cam's corner. "With whom?"

I've always been a stickler about the usage of *who* and *whom*, much to the chagrin of all my friends and family, whom I am incessantly correcting.

"With everyone," said Smitty. "Or everyone that matters, anyway. Talk about your observations and ideas with your team, for example. 'Here's what I'm noticing. What are you seeing?' That kind of thing. Just kick it around and see where the discussion takes you. See what happens over time."

Cam stared at him, slack-jawed. "Talk with my team about... nothing? What are we, *Seinfeld* now?" he choked. "When? During all that spare time we have on our hands? Right! Hey everybody, hang up those phones! Let someone else close those loans for a while so we can go out for lattes and talk about nothing! Are you crazy? Don't answer that."

"You're not talking about nothing; you're talking about everything. Everything you've been observing and thinking about. And you're not doing this to waste time; you're doing this to create new ideas, new ways of serving your customers, and new ways of getting more business. Ultimately, that's what this is all about, Cam, and that's what you really want, isn't it?"

"Yeah, but I don't see how."

"Because you're too dang *linear*, that's why." Smitty interrupted. "You have to give this some time and eventually, and I'll write you a personal guarantee on this, a new idea's gonna pop up and WUP you upside the head. There's no way to know where it's gonna come from. There's no way to predict which conversation will lead to what new idea. But it will happen. You hearin' me?"

"Hearin', just not believin'," Cam replied with a mocking Texas drawl.

"I'm tellin' ya, dude. It'll happen. I mean, back in 1966, Herb Kelleher sketched out the idea for Southwest Airlines on the back of a napkin, for gosh sakes. One day he and his pal Rollin King just started talking and WUP! There it was."

"That's not the same thing," sniffed Cam.

Smitty leaned forward in his chair and slid his wallet out of the back pocket of his cargo shorts. He plucked a wad of bills from inside, rifled through it for a moment, and slapped a crisp, one-hundred-dollar note on the table in front of Cam. "Go on," he said. "Take it."

Cam reluctantly dragged the bill toward himself, rolling his eyes. "What's the catch?"

"Start using the WUP just like I been describing it to ya. Do it for a month. Have weekly discussions with your team. Do it even though you think it's an inane idea from a loony old coot."

"And?" Cam was eyeing the C-note.

"And I'll give you ten more of them Franklins just for playin' the game."

I did what they call in the movies a spit-take and spewed coffee on the table. "You're going to pay him a thousand bucks to take your advice?" I cried.

"$1,100, actually," said Cam.

"But you gotta promise me one thing," Smitty continued, ignoring me. "When inspiration strikes, when a new, bona fide really great idea presents itself—"

"Yeah?"

"You have to do it; that's number six. That's when the talking comes to a screeching halt and audacious action takes over. Kelleher and King went from idea to Southwest's first route map on the back of that napkin. In other words, my man, I am expecting you to stick your neck out and try something new in your business. Got it?"

"And," Cam folded the bill and stuck it in his shirt pocket, "what if I don't?"

"Then you keep the hundred," Smitty offered. "And the knowledge that you, the big-shot dealmaker, super sales guy, wasn't up to this one itty-bitty task. And Farber and I will know the truth about Cameron Summerfield, that he dresses up like a big, strong mover and shaker, but he's really a mewling little boy in short pants and knee socks."

I laughed, I couldn't help it, but so did Cam, which I thought was a pretty good sign. He said, "Deal," and patted the pocket on his finely woven cotton and silk blend shirt.

Smitty turned his attention on me. "Are you getting the full picture here, Farberama? Do you see where the WUP can lead?"

"Yeah, I do. I'm going to give it a try myself."

"Of course you are," he grunted. "And I ain't paying you, so don't even ask. But here's the full picture. Can you imagine, Farber, what it would be like for an entire company to have everybody—and by everybody, I mean *everybody* from the CEO to the receptionist—keep his or her own Wake-Up Pad? And every so often—weekly, monthly, it really doesn't matter—there's a meeting where all that happens is people compare notes and talk about what they're seeing. Then when the ideas start flyin', you capture 'em, and you start trying stuff. That would be a whole company of CIOs. A company that is entirely awake to what's happening outside its walls. Can you imagine that, Farberoni?"

I could imagine it and it brought to mind what Gary Hamel said in his book, *Leading the Revolution*: "Every day, companies get blindsided by the future—yet the future never arrives as a surprise to everyone in the organization. Someone somewhere was paying attention." An entire company of people paying attention. When I really stopped and thought about it, I was damn near awestruck by the potential.

So, I wrote the idea in *my* WUP, which at the moment was a crumpled napkin.

I jotted down the words *Carry, Scan, Eavesdrop, Ponder, Talk, and Try Something New,* and then wrote, *everyone a CIO? How? What could happen?* I turned to Cam, a vision of millions of CIOs swimming in my head, and asked what he thought of all this.

"Not now...I'm scanning," he said as he watched a group of startlingly attractive young women walking in a bevy on the beach.

Smitty put his hand on my shoulder and laughed, "Buddy, you got yourself a live one here."

Then, as if goosed by an invisible elf, Smitty jumped up and reached into another of his many cargo pockets. "Hey, I nearly forgot," he said as he rooted about. "Got something for you that I think you're gonna like." He pulled out a folded envelope and handed it to me.

I took it from him and looked it over, front and back. There was no address, return or otherwise.

"I meant to give it to you when we sat down," he said. "But we got all distracted and whatnot. Anyway, you need to read it right now. He said it was real important."

"Who did?"

Smitty grinned. "It's from Edg."

12.

My heart skipped when I recognized the script. I hadn't heard from Edg in the two years since he'd swept into my world and in one eventful week twisted my head and heart around until I got my life back on track. He had opened my eyes to the nature of Extreme Leadership and what it meant to take the Radical Leap—cultivate love, generate energy, inspire audacity, and provide proof; insight that had helped me beyond measure. Then, just as suddenly as he'd swooped into my life, he was gone. "Big waves await me at other shores," he had said with his typical, annoying cryptic aplomb. Now he was back, in the form of scratchy blue ink on yellow legal paper. I excused myself from the table and walked down to the shore to spend a few moments catching up with my old friend.

> *Dear Steve,*
>
> *The beach I'm sitting on is whiter than talcum and, this time of year, cooler than cool as the sand runs over my feet and through my toes. The waves are perfect here, dude, and the mist coming off the ocean is almost enough to spray away my grief over Pops. But I don't want it to, you know? He was my mentor, my friend, my—is this a word?— shaper. It'll take a hell of a lot more than sea spit to get my mind off him.*
>
> *It's weird, but I can see him so vividly now that he's gone. Pops left me memories. And feelings. And—okay, I'll say it—a boatload of money. Not that I need it. But the lessons, dude...well...you can imagine.*
>
> *Pops taught everyone he touched how important it is to take the radical leap, and there's no doubt that*

*that knowledge will be at the core of his legacy. Pops
was the champion of audacity, of the need to have a
bold and blatant disregard for normal constraints.
But most important was his deep, unwavering de-
votion to the plight of the human condition and the
challenge, joy, and, ultimately, responsibility of the
human experience. To be an Extreme Leader, Pops
would say, is really nothing more than the challenge
to be fully human at work, at home, in the community,
and in the world as a whole. And, according to him,
to be fully human means that you accept a radical
level of personal accountability for making the future
markedly better than the present.*

*Accountability has become an uncomfortable
idea; it's that thing that people desperately want other
people to take. These people need to be more accountable is an edict that I've heard more times than
I care to remember. Pops's message is this: you are
accountable. You. Whoever you are. Do you need to
enlist other people? Of course. Do you have to make
things happen all by your little lonesome? Of course
not. Pops didn't build an empire by himself. But he
held himself accountable for everything he ever set
out to accomplish. And everything he ever set out to
accomplish would, if successful, change some piece
of the world he touched for the better. That level of
accountability, dude, is not simply about being more
effective and productive at work. It's not just about
achieving goals and accomplishing tasks, and it's not
about proving to anyone how wonderful a person you*

are. It's about living, breathing, toiling, and playing
way the hell out there on that radical edge where you
simultaneously stoke your business to phenomenal
success, amp your life to the loudest possible volume
of joy and meaning, and change the world for all of
us. Hit all three things at the same time and you've
got the Radical Edge as a businessperson and as a
human being.

I've been thinking about you, Farber. You and I
have a unique connection, and Pops certainly saw
something in you, too. So I've been wondering: are you
just thinking about Extreme Leadership, or are you
ready to skate out on the Radical Edge? I hope you are
because if all you want to do is enhance your perfor-
mance, then burn this letter and go take a class at The
Learning Annex.

Agnes used to say, "If you live in this world without
ever attempting to change it, you will have sold a ruby
for the price of Spam."

That's Agnes. She's a ruby if ever there was one.
She owns a diner near the beach in Encinitas called
The Wake-Up Call. I spent a lot of hours there when I
was a kid, hanging out there under Agnes's watchful
eye whenever Pops was traveling, which was pretty
damn often. She was a woman who lived on the
Radical Edge, and, believe it or not, Pops learned a
great deal from her. And so did I. And guess what, so
will you.

You need to go talk to Agnes, Farber. Today. Go
directly to The Wake-Up Call. Do not pass go; do not

collect two hundred dollars. I've asked Smitty to point
you in the right direction. You're gonna love her and
I'm sure the feeling will be mutual. Oh, and one more
thing: Don't forget your WUP.

Later dude.

Love, Edg

13.

I folded the note and put it in my pocket as I walked back up the
beach to rejoin Smitty and Cam at the café. I was thrilled to hear
from Edg, and I was excited about meeting this woman, Agnes.
She had to be an exceedingly special person to have had such an
influence on Edg and Pops. I admit that I would have preferred
visiting Agnes alone, but since I'd committed myself to Cam for
the day, I reluctantly decided to bring him along. As I got to the
table, I noticed that my two dudes seemed to be tolerating each
other well enough. Nothing appeared broken, anyway.

"Well, Cam, it looks like we have a lunch date up in Encinitas."

Smitty clapped his hands, pushed his chair back, and jumped
to his feet. "You boys are in for a treat. Agnes Golden is one of
a kind, and that's a shame for the rest of us. We could use a lot
more just like her, that's for sure."

"Who is she?" asked Cam.

"You'll see, Buck. Even you won't be able to resist her charms."

Cam looked at me.

I shook my head. "I don't know her either, Cam, but let's just
say she comes highly recommended. And besides, we're going
to have to eat lunch anyway, so why not at The Wake-Up Call?"

"From the Wake-Up Pad to The Wake-Up Call, huh? Is that a coincidence, or does everyone in your circle of friends have a fear of sleep?"

"No co-inky-dink, Buck. Agnes named 'em both."

"Well, then," said Cam the all-knowing sales god. "I'm sure this *will* be a treat."

Agnes

14.

The Wake-Up Call was on the main drag of Encinitas, just two blocks from the ocean. It felt like a small beach community diner but with an impressively brisk lunch business. As I searched for a parking space and scanned the bumpers of the parked cars for the telltale backup light, I noticed that the tables on the sidewalk were packed. The inside clearly was, too, because another crowd was hovering in front of the adjacent boutiques, waiting for their turn.

As luck would have it, and sometimes you're just lucky, I found a spot three blocks south. Cam had suggested that I park closer in a delivery zone and that he'd pay the inevitable ticket to save time. Even though that was an interesting take on valet parking, I decided to play it legal. Besides, a short walk wouldn't hurt either of us.

As we sauntered up the crowded sidewalk toward the diner, I gathered The Wake-Up Call's clientele wasn't the normal touristy bunch. Conversations throughout the patio were in full lunchtime swing and the wait staff moved effortlessly among the tables with plates of food, pots of coffee, and lots of laughter. I got the distinct impression that they all knew each other.

We made our way inside and found the hostess, who was dressed in a flowered T-shirt and khaki shorts and wrapped in a white apron with a name badge that said Mary Ellen in a friendly, festive script. Her blonde hair was pulled back from her perfectly tanned face. She appeared to be in her early forties, although with her lithe, runner's frame and youthful, energetic demeanor, it wouldn't surprise me if she got carded every now and then.

"Hey, boys, welcome to The Wake-Up Call," she virtually sang. "We've got about a thirty-minute wait right now. Shall I put you on the list for something inside, outside, or the first one that pops up?"

"Actually," I ventured, looking around at the throngs of diners, "Edg sent us to see Agnes. Any chance you can get us in?" Name-dropping never hurts, although I always feel a little guilty trying it.

"Oh, that boy!" Mary Ellen chirped. "I haven't seen him since Pops left us. How is he?"

"He seems to be doing fine." True, as far as I knew. "I'm sure he'd appreciate your asking about him. Is Agnes here?"

"First time at The Wake-Up Call, eh? She's in the back booth, as always. And it looks like she's alone, which is very unusual. Can I bring you a..." she sized us up and then pointed a finger at me and said, "a Diet Coke and," a finger at Cam, "a black coffee?"

"Yeah, sure," I said, surprised as Cam nodded in agreement. "How'd you know?"

"Just a little game I like to play. It's no big thing, I'm wrong as often as I'm right, but it doesn't stop me from guessing," she laughed with a disarming burst of joy. "Come with me; I'll tell her you're here."

As she walked us toward the back booth, I saw a tall, slightly plump African-American woman sitting peacefully in a cushioned bench against the wall. As we got closer I realized that "peaceful" was something of an understatement. She was, in fact, sleeping. Her chin slumped slightly toward her chest, and her short, otherwise thick, gray hair was thinning slightly on top, which I knew because that was pretty much all I could see of her as we approached. I marveled at how anyone could take a nap in the middle of all this chaos. Mary Ellen put her hand gently on Sleeping Beauty's shoulder and she straightened immediately, blinking her eyes as though being aroused from a deep thought rather than a slumber. She had to be at least ninety years old, which for some reason caught me entirely off guard. Her dark face was deeply lined, and white, meticulously plucked eyebrows arched playfully over her gray, luminous eyes. "A couple of young studs here to see you, Agnes," Mary Ellen winked at us. "Should I send them away?"

"Oh, you're so bad, girl." Agnes raised her perfect eyebrows at Mary Ellen as she chuckled. She looked Cam and me over as though sizing us up against that stud remark and then gestured for us to sit. I slid into the booth and Cam followed.

Smiling with her whole face, Agnes extended her delicate hand across the table and, feeling myself melting, I took it in mine. "And you are Farber. Don't look so shocked, Smitty called to say you were coming. I know you have a first name, baby, so why do Edg and Smitty call you *Farber*?"

"Not unusual," I said, loving that she called me *baby*.

"Most people know me on a last name basis, I guess."

"Well, *Steve's* gonna work just fine for me." She turned toward Cam, who'd been conspicuously silent so far. "And who's this handsome young man?"

Before I could make the introduction, Cam thrust out his hand and said, "I am the prisoner, he is the warden, and this," he swept his head around to indicate his surroundings, "is my jail."

Agnes looked at Cam's hand and hesitated ever so slightly before she gripped it in both of hers. "Oh, my," she smiled. "My, my, my."

You got that right, I thought/mumbled to myself.

"Call me Cam, though. Cam Summerfield." He shot Agnes such a charming grin that I almost yelped in surprise. This dude could certainly turn on the charm when he wanted to. It almost seemed—and I mean almost—that he felt guilty about spewing his sarcasm on this innocent old lady.

Mary Ellen arrived with my Diet Coke and Cam's coffee. I picked up my glass and took a sip; Cam did the same with his coffee, except he used his left hand, which almost caused us to have a midair beverage collision.

"You're a lefty," I said to Cam as Mary Ellen stood by the table. "I never noticed that before."

"You got a problem with *that*, now?" he sneered.

"No, he doesn't," said Mary Ellen in my defense. "He's just being observant, right?"

"Right," I said. "Just like you." I wondered if she'd read the same book I had.

"That, my friend," said the hostess to Cam, "is a lefthanded coffee cup."

Yep. We'd read the same book, all right. Hal Rosenbluth, the travel executive, had once written a story about a waitress who would size up her customers and then serve drinks to the left side of her lefty guests. It was a great lesson in adapting to the needs of customers and not expecting them to adapt to yours, and I hadn't thought about it for many years. It was cool to see someone actually putting it into practice.

Cam picked up the cup and gave it a dubious perusal. "Sorry. I don't see the difference."

"You've never heard of the left-handed cup factory?" asked Agnes.

"No. Can't say I have." Cam peered at her over the thick ceramic mug.

"There's a good reason for that," she said.

"Which is?"

"There isn't one, you silly young man."

We all had a good laugh at Cam's expense, which I have to admit, I very much enjoyed.

"I'll explain it to you later, southpaw," I said, patting his hand, and immediately regretting my patronizing tone.

Cam put the cup down and rolled his eyes toward the ceiling. Mary Ellen walked away, chuckling under her breath, while Agnes reached across the table and laid her delicate, veined hand on Cam's. "I'm sorry, Cam. That was very rude of us, but I assure you that it wasn't meanspirited. Will you forgive us?" She went on to explain Rosenbluth's story. "That kind of observant, do it for the customer before they ask approach is just the way we do business here at The Wake-Up Call. I've done it that way my entire life. And that's ninety-plus years."

"But who's counting?" I chimed in.

"I am," she said. "Every blessed minute."

I let that sink in for a moment. "With respect, Agnes," I said. "There's clearly something very special about you and your diner."

"Thank you," she smiled.

"You're welcome, but that's not where I was going. For some

reason, Edg sent me here to talk to you, but—and again I mean no disrespect—but why? I mean, I've eaten in a lot of great diners and restaurants but there's got to be something more to this; am I right?"

"Well, yes. There's always something more than what meets the naked eye, true?"

"True, but…" I was trying to think of a polite way to ask the question, but I was striking out. "To put it bluntly, Agnes, who are you and why are we here?"

Much to my relief, she laughed and said that she'd be happy to tackle the first part of the question. "But first things first," she said and waggled her fingers in the air to catch Mary Ellen's attention. She nodded at Agnes and then disappeared into the kitchen just as another server appeared at our table to refill our drinks. A few minutes later—it seemed like seconds, really—Mary Ellen returned with platters of sliced pastrami, roast beef, ham, and turkey, three kinds of cheese, french fries, onion rings, rolls, bread, condiments, potato salad, coleslaw and crisp, kosher dills. Cam and I stared in stunned silence.

"The Agnes special," Mary Ellen said with a smile. "Help yourselves, fellas."

Believe me, we did. As I assembled my first sandwich, Agnes began her story. And I enjoyed every blessed minute.

15.

Agnes Golden grew up in Chicago in a middle-class, black family who had high hopes that she would apply her terrific intellect and relentless drive to the practice of medicine. For as long as

Agnes could remember, however, and to the shock and horror of her parents, she wanted to be a foodie. She wanted her own bar, restaurant, café, or even a hotdog stand on the pier at Lake Michigan. She wanted to make simple comfort food, serve it to fanatically loyal customers, and revel in the reputation that could only come through a truly inspired and mystical bowl of chili.

When she was in the fifth grade, she would fantasize about turning her family's home into a burger joint with very limited and exclusive seating and a celebrated reputation for the most sublime, and coveted, secret sauce in the city of Chicago. As she experimented in the kitchen she would imagine the crowds lining up along her street, waiting for hours with great anticipation for a precious seat at one of three tables set in the small living room.

That childhood fantasy stayed with her on some subtle, pre-conscious level all the way up through grade school, middle school, high school (where she was a star volleyball player), college, and even through her first year of medical school. The pressure of being a female African-American med student in those days was significant, to say the least, and Agnes found her grades sliding down to average and her mind drifting more and more frequently back to her restaurant dreams.

She helped pay her way through school by waiting tables, which was no shock to anyone in her family, but when the excruciating time demands of med school forced her to choose between her restaurant job and poking at cadavers for a C average at best, she quit school. The irony of her quitting med school nearly causing her father a heart attack was not entirely lost on her. But it also didn't stop her from begging her dad for the money to finally start her own business and bring to fruition that small seed that so many of us leave buried in the soil of our childhood memories.

Agnes's Real Chicago Hot Dog and Chili Palace was born and the first menu-fliers printed on Agnes's twentieth birthday. Thirty-one years later, she sold her chain of twenty-one Palaces, and, at the wheezy old age of fifty-something, having achieved the rarified status of Chicago restaurant maven, moved to San Diego to retire.

She bought a big house in Del Mar overlooking the ocean and spent her days hanging out on the beach and learning to surf from some of the local legends, who became her second family.

"But old foodies never die," she said, picking a crisp onion ring from the wicker basket. "So I bought this little building and opened The Wake-Up Call so I could feed my friends and make a little money while I was at it. Just for fun, you know."

"Excuse me," said Cam. "Just so I'm clear on this. You're loaded, aren't you?"

I practically choked on my cheddar roll and for a panicked moment hoped that Dr. Heimlich was in the house.

"Cam!" I croaked. "What the...?"

"*What*?" he exclaimed. "I'm just asking a question. You *are*, right?"

"I've done very well. Yes, baby, I have done very, very well."

She was the embodiment of graciousness. As far as I was concerned. I'd have clobbered Cam with a cast-iron skillet, if I were Agnes. Although I did have to give the boy points for focus, in that lovely story of Agnes's pursuit of her lifelong dream, all Cam saw was the payday. There could never be a drop of doubt that money was his prime boat floater.

16.

"It's all about the money for you, isn't it, Cam?" I said with rising vexation. "Isn't there anything else that turns you on? Anything?"

"Look," Cam said with an appetizing mouthful of coleslaw. "You're supposed to be helping me with my business, aren't you?"

I took a bite of my sandwich.

"Well, aren't you?" he persisted.

I turned to Agnes and explained the circumstances that had brought Cam and me together for the day, though I left out the details about the precariousness of Cam's employment situation. "Yeah, of course," I answered, setting my food back on the plate. "That's the general idea, sure."

"It's not the *general* idea; it's the *whole* idea. And business is about making money. That's it. No money, no profit, no business. Game over; end of story." He kept his eyes on mine but pointed a finger at Agnes. "This nice old lady here—no offense, Agnes—has obviously made tons of money. Don't even pretend that's not important, because it is. Jeez, Farber. It's almost like you think she should apologize for it."

"I'm just saying," I frothed, "that you should open up your freakin' eyes to other..."

With a surprising burst of energy, Agnes sat up and reached her hands across the table. Like a mother intervening in her children's sib spat, she grabbed each of us by the chin and pulled our faces toward her so we were both looking her in the eye. She didn't let go and—okay, I'll admit it—it started to hurt. I can't imagine what this scene must have looked like to the other customers, and when someone across the diner laughed, I was certain it was at us.

"Boys," Agnes said in a controlled voice. "It's time for you both to, and I mean this in the nicest way, shut the hell up." It was as though this gentle, innocent old lady had morphed before my eyes into a steely disciplinarian. Still clenching our chins in her sinewy fingers, she began, once again, to smile. She let go and gave each of us a pat on the cheek.

"May I speak?" It wasn't really a question. "Thank you. Cam is right, Steve. I'm proud of the money I've made over my lifetime. There is no point in starting a business, whether it's a restaurant, or a—what is it you do again?"

"I sell mortgages."

"Right, mortgages. Whether it's a restaurant, or a mortgage company, or a carpet cleaning operation, or a pharmaceutical company, the business has to make money. And the more the better, I say."

"Well, there you go," said a triumphant Cam with a wave of his fork. "That's what I'm saying."

"Steve?" She raised her eyebrows at me. "Care to chime in?"

"You just told me to shut the hell up, as I recall."

"Yes, I guess I did," she laughed. "So I guess I'll continue, then. Cam?"

"Agnes?"

"You're pretty successful, right?"

"I'm the best." The boy just oozed humility.

"Make a lot of money, do you, baby?"

"Never enough."

"Never enough," she repeated. "And where does your money come from?"

He took another bite of coleslaw. "Selling mortgages, like I said."

"Mmmm...hmmm," she mused. "And where would you guess mine comes from?"

"That's obvious. Selling food."

"I want you to look around this diner," she said gesturing her hand at the room. "And tell me what you see."

"I see people having lunch."

Agnes eyed him. "Oh, come on now, sugar. Tell me what you see."

He slowed his glance around the room slightly. "OK, there are people talking and laughing and eating and there are waitresses doing the same."

"And how many tables are empty?"

Cam craned his neck around. "Well, none, that I can see."

"That's right. Not an empty table in the house, and there rarely is. Do you know why?"

He shrugged matter-of-factly. "Food's good."

"Thank you. Anything else?"

"Price is right."

"And?"

Cam's face betrayed that he was drawing a blank. "Does it look like people are enjoying themselves, Cam?" Agnes prompted.

"Yeah, I guess."

"How about all those people waiting outside?"

"What about them?" I finally chimed in.

"Do they look miserable?" She didn't wait for an answer. "No! They look happy, don't they?"

It was true. Everyone—whether eating at a table, waiting for food, or standing in line—seemed genuinely cheerful. It was kind of odd, now that I'd noticed it. Odd in a wonderful way.

"I'm going to tell you why they're happy, Cam. I'm going to tell you why, since the day I opened my first Hot Dog Palace, people keep coming back and spending their money with me and mine. I'm going to tell you why, Cam, but you're not going to believe me."

"Try me," he said in a patient, almost patronizing, tone.

"It's because I love them," whispered Agnes.

17.

I'd heard this theme before from Pops, of course. I'd been struggling with his mantra, "Do what you love in the service of people who love what you do," and trying to put it into practice in my own life and business. So it was a little jarring when I heard what Agnes said next:

"This is how you stoke the fires of your success, Cam, by doing what you love in the service of people you love, who, in turn, love what you do for them."

"Uh-huh," muttered Cam. "So you're honestly telling me that you love every single individual human being that ever stepped into one of your restaurants for the last seventy-some-odd years."

I thought he laid out the challenge quite well, actually.

That's exactly the thing that I was wrestling with, too. I sat up and leaned forward to hear Agnes's response.

"I wish I could tell you that," she said, folding her hands on the table. "I wish I could say that I have a heart big enough and a mind clear enough of judgment to embrace nothing but the goodness in every single person on this planet, saint and sinner alike. But I can't."

"So what *are* you saying then?" I asked before Cam had a chance to throw a barb.

"Well, it's really pretty straightforward, boys."

"That's not the word I was thinking," said Cam.

"Think what you will, honey, but it is really very practical. I may not have the capacity to love everyone, but I certainly do have the capacity to act as though I do and to run my business accordingly. And if I and my team can really do that, then no other business in my market space can come close to the experience that we give our customers."

Cam set his fork down. "Then explain something to me, please. How come I make so much money?"

Agnes tilted her head at him. "Why don't you tell me?"

"Yes, I will." He leaned back in the booth and laced his hands behind his head. "It's not lovey-dovey, I'll tell you that. I work my ass off; no one works harder than I do. In at 6:30 a.m., out at 10 p.m. most days. When I was a sales agent I'd make hundreds of calls, and if no leads were coming in, I'd go through the damn phone book if I had to. My business is all about the transaction, the loan. I close the deal and someone else takes it from there. It's a numbers game and nothing else. And I've always generated more numbers than anybody."

"Wow, you have a great work ethic, to say the least," said Agnes with all sincerity. "And you must get a lot of referral business."

The comment stopped him for a moment and he shifted in his seat. "Nah. Don't need it."

Agnes paused. "And you're a manager, right?"

"Senior vice president of sales. Youngest of the execs," he beamed.

"That's something to be very proud of," she said, again, with total genuineness.

He was aglow, getting all warm and toasty inside as his ego expanded. "Yep."

"So, how about your sales team? Do they work as hard as you do?"

Cam grunted. "I wish. But I pump 'em pretty hard to get it all done."

"I'll bet you do, sugar. And they'd follow you through thick and thin, wouldn't they?"

Uh-oh, I thought. *Here it comes.* I had a feeling that Cam's balloon was about to go blammo.

Cam appeared to have divine intervention on his side because just then Mary Ellen stopped by to refill our drinks. She set her order pad on the table and whispered something in Agnes's ear. Agnes nodded, and Mary Ellen scurried away, leaving her order pad behind.

"She," said Agnes watching Mary Ellen, "is priceless. She helped me open this place and has been here ever since. Single mom, accomplished athlete, extraordinary businessperson. She runs the place now, but back when she was waiting tables, customers would wait in line just to get into her section. You know why?"

"She's fast?" said Cam, clearly happy to change the subject.

"I've seen faster, to tell the truth. In fact, sometimes she can be pretty slow turning tables over. So it's not because she's fast—but we were talking about you, weren't we? Oh yes, thick and thin, right? So how about it, Cam?"

Cam pretended not to know what she was asking. "How about what?"

"Why won't your team follow you?"

"I never said that." He was starting to smolder, and I was

tempted to order a basket of popcorn to munch on while the fireworks went off.

"But it's true. I can tell by the way you're avoiding the question, baby. And also because you have to—how did you say it—pump them pretty hard to get results. They do what you tell them to do because you're the boss. They perform because they have to; not because they want to. In other words, Cam, you're not a leader at all; you're a taskmaster."

Cam bristled in his seat. "Wait a minute. Hold on. I'm not sitting around and barking orders while I'm relaxing under a coconut tree or something. I'm slammin' it harder than they are. I demand no more of them than what I demand of myself."

"Wrong!" Agnes erupted. "Wrong, wrong, wrong!" She slapped her palm on the table.

Everything stopped and heads turned in the diner. I was stunned to hear such thunder emit from this sweet old lady. When Mary Ellen looked back at us over her shoulder and shook her head as if to say *there she goes again*, however, I got the impression that an occasional Agnes cloudburst was to be expected.

"I want you to tell me right now why you work as hard as you do," she railed. "Tell me why you work those long hours, make all those calls, go to all those meetings, close all those loans. Tell me!"

Cam sat blown back in his seat with a startled expression on his face that I hadn't yet seen or even thought he was capable of making. His mouth was moving, but it took a moment for him to get any words out.

"It's my job," he sputtered. "It's how I get paid."

"And?" Agnes pressed.

"And it's a rush, it's a blast."

"And you love it," I said before I could stop myself. "You love the game, don't you Cam?"

"Yeah. Okay. Fine. There's nothing better," he said again with eyes rolling.

"Oh, yes there is," said Agnes, as if he were serious. "Yes there is, indeed."

18.

It's funny how things work. As I look back on the trajectory of my own life, it seems to me that all the things I've done and all the people I've met have yielded lessons that have built on each other in increasingly meaningful ways. Some are convinced that the human experience is random and our time on this earth is not only infinitesimal but insignificant as well, the *life's-a-bitch-and-then-you-die* school of thought. I'm not much of a philosopher, so don't ask me to argue the finer points of this age-old debate between meaning and meaninglessness, but it sure looks to me as though life serves up one lesson after another, and, just when I think I've got it nailed, got it all figured out, I come to realize that I am, in fact, an idiot.

I had told Rich Delacroix that I like everybody. Sure, I'd been exaggerating a tad, but, compared to most people it was true. It takes a lot for me to dislike someone. Really, it does. I've had plenty of conflict, argument, and misunderstanding in my life, and some relationships that had started well ended badly. I've had a failed business partnership and a failed marriage, so I know what it feels like when someone lets you down and vice versa. Still, my shit list is very, very short. In fact, I pride myself on my ability to look into the eyes of another human being and find something in there to like, to appreciate, maybe even to embrace. That, I believed, is what made me a good leadership coach.

On that day, however, sitting across from that gem of a woman in her marvelous little diner, I realized just how far it was I had to go. She was starting to get tough on Cam, but she never gave the slightest hint, the faintest inkling that she was just tolerating or putting up with him as a favor to someone else. She invested herself completely in this little bag of wind just as I, to my dismay, was good and ready to write him off. *What does this say about me?* I was asking myself as Agnes was asking Cam an oddly similar question. The cloudburst had passed just as suddenly as it had begun.

"What would they say about you, Cam?"

"What would who say?"

"Well," she said, "let's start with your direct reports, your sales managers."

He poked his fork into a pickle. "Not a fair question. You'll have to ask them."

"All right, fair enough. But seeing as how they're not here, what do *you* say they'd say about you?" Again, the warmhearted smile to contrast my increasing need for Zantac. And believe me, it wasn't a food related need.

"They'd say I'm hard on them. They'd say I have no tolerance for laziness. Most of all, they'd say that I bring on the results."

"And your peers would say?"

"Okay," he fished his business card from his wallet and flicked it across the table. "Look at the title; that says it all, as far as I'm concerned."

She left it there without giving it the slightest glance. "And your customers?" Agnes asked patiently.

"What?"

"Your customers, Cam. Those people that bought you your car, what would they say about you?"

"How the hell am I supposed to know that? Listen, Agnes," he crunched the end of the pickle skewered on his fork, "I get my customers a rate that they're happy with and a program that'll give me the highest possible fees and commissions without hurting them. I do it fast and I do it right and that's the end of that. Everybody's satisfied. What else is there to know?"

"Okay, then!" she exclaimed and pushed herself up from the booth. I was amazed at her height: around six feet—a good inch or two taller than I am. She stood steady as a rock and looked down at us with hands on her hips. "Don't go away. I need to go talk with someone for a moment, but I'll be right back. I'll have Mary Ellen bring you some dessert, and when I return," she stared down at Cam, "It'll be your turn to listen to me. Got that, baby?"

She turned and was gone before Cam could respond.

19.

"And Judge Judy retires to consider her verdict," Cam smirked. He did that a lot.

"Listen, Cam," I began. "I promised Rich that I'd spend the day with you, get to know you a bit, but I gotta tell you..."

Mary Ellen, again with impeccable timing, swooped by, cleared the platters, and set in the middle of the table a plate with an outrageous, ginormous piece of chocolate cake. It had an inch-thick layer of glistening icing with a swirl jutting from the top as if it were flipping the bird to Dr. Atkins.

I picked up one of the two forks and sank it into the cake, helpless against the sweet siren song of the carbohydrates. "Oh, baby," I said; momentarily forgetting that Cam even existed. "This is worth the trip."

"You gotta tell me what?" Cam asked as he followed suit with his own fork.

"Hmmm?"

"You said, 'but I gotta tell ya...' You gotta tell me what?"

"I'm not sure this is going to work out, you and me."

"That's fine by me, Steve." He started to get up, but I grasped his wrist and motioned for him to stay.

"Look, Cam," I breathed. "We really need to try to get through the day. As much as I hate to say it, we both stand to gain something from this, especially you."

"Excuse me?"

"Bluntly, Cam? Your job depends on it."

"Is that a threat?" He fished for his cell. "Let's just call Rich right now and that'll be that."

Again, I grabbed his wrist. "Not a good idea. Trust me on that. Let's just give this thing another go, all right? I'm curious about what Agnes has to say, aren't you?"

Cam's wheels were turning and he looked a little shaken, as if he was beginning to realize that his situation might not be quite as rosy as he thought.

Then he did something that blew my mind right out its socket. It may very well have been the last thing I expected Cam to do at that moment.

He took out his WUP and began to write.

Fascination, Gratitude, and Thou

20.

I tried to peer over Cam's shoulder, but he created a barrier with his arms as if blocking a cheating neighbor during a high school exam. I kept my mouth shut and let him scribble, which he was doing furiously. Suddenly I had the sense that someone was watching us and turned my head to see Agnes standing behind our booth, looking at Cam with a satisfied smile.

"Is that a Wake-Up Pad, baby?"

Cam jumped and turned his head as well. "Yeah, well, something to do while we were waiting for you." He slapped shut the notebook and started to stuff it back in his pocket. "Keep it out, please, Cam," she said as she slid back into the booth. "You may want to take some notes." She turned her gaze to me and raised her eyebrows questioningly.

"Ummm...well...I haven't gotten around to picking one up yet," I told her. "I've got a tablet at home that'll do the trick, but I haven't been there since this morning."

She picked up Mary Ellen's order pad, which had been sitting at the end of the table. "Here, use this."

"But that's..."

"Just take it." She pushed it to me across the linoleum tabletop.

It was fresh and unmarked and as I flipped through the glue-bound pages, it was clear that this was not your typical server tool. The first half of the pad had the words *Scan & Eavesdrop* printed along the top of each page, followed by several pages with the heading *Ponder*. Farther back, another series said *Talking Points*, and the leaves in the final section each carried the heading of *Try This*.

"That's Mary Ellen's own design," said Agnes. "And it has to do with one of the many reasons that young woman is so extraordinary. Mary Ellen makes it her solemn mission to get to know—I mean really know—everyone who sits in her section. To the point where," she tapped on Cam's hand, "she'll know what side to serve the coffee on.

"She doesn't always succeed, mind you, and it does take her longer to turn over a table, but you know what happens? Her customers love her so much that they come back again and again, and will keep coming back as long as Mary Ellen is alive and well and working at The Wake-Up Call."

"So where does the pad come in?" I asked, flipping, once again, through the pages.

"Simple, really," Agnes beamed as though bragging about a favorite daughter. "She doesn't have to write orders, carries it all in her head. So, instead, she treats every customer encounter as an exercise in fascination. They think she's writing down their orders, but she's really capturing little gems of conversation and behavior—little nuggets of humanity. She may look like she's just waitressing or hostessing, but she's not."

Cam was clearly trying to get his mind around this. "Then what is she doing?"

"She's pursuing the Radical Edge, sweetheart. Her WUP is just the tool to get her there and keep her there."

"And there is where, exactly?" I asked, trying to recall what Edg had said in his letter.

"The Radical Edge is that zone of total value, total *significance* to one's self and to others. It's about achieving the simultaneous fulfillment of three of life's seemingly incompatible spheres."

Something had shifted in Agnes's tone. I was getting a glimpse behind Oz's curtain and seeing Her Wizardness for what she really was. Sure, she was a successful entrepreneur; sure, she was a kind though stern motherly figure but above all, I now saw, she was a philosopher who thought very deeply about things and took those thoughts very seriously. "Your business, your personal life, and your effect on the world," she said. "When you're hitting on those three cylinders simultaneously, you've achieved the Radical Edge and life takes on an entirely new level of meaning."

"Smitty gave us a tutorial on WUPing this morning, but I think you've just put it in context for me," I said, stroking my chin in a scholarly manner. It's the only scholarly manner I have, come to think of it.

"Oh, yes, well, Smitty...Smitty is a WUP master," she chuckled at her description. "But that's not exactly a coincidence, my friends," said Agnes. She leaned in with a conspiratorial twinkle in her eyes. "I'm the one that started Billy Maritime down this road many, many years ago, and Billy taught it to Smitty when he was just a young pup like you, Cam."

Excuse me? "You taught this to Pops?" I don't know why I was stunned, but I was. "How did that happen? I mean, how were you two connected? You know what I mean." I was all but stammering.

"It was nothing formal, Steve. At first, he was my customer. He'd come in here with little Theodore—sorry, Edg—and our friendship just developed over the years. We did a lot of talking, that's all. Do enough talking, for enough years, and you're bound to not only learn from each other, but also help each other out along the way. He was the real genius; I just kind of goosed him along." She paused for a moment, obviously lost in reverie, and then let out a deep, trembling sigh. "Don't ever let anyone tell you that customers are just customers. If that'd been my attitude, I'd have missed out on one of my life's greatest treasures: Billy 'Pops' Maritime and his little boy, Edg."

I don't know if she'd meant to, but Agnes had baited the hook, tossed it into the pond, and jerked the line with perfect finesse. Cam was snagged. For him, merely mentioning the Maritime name made Agnes ripple with credibility; the fact that she knew Pops so well made her virtually irresistible. That's pretty much how I felt, too.

Agnes snapped back to the present. "But you're not here to talk about the Family Maritime, are you?"

"Works for me!" I exclaimed.

"Some other time, Steve." She responded looking at Cam, who met her eyes with full attention, pen at the ready in his left hand. That was a first, and it was clear that Agnes was going to take full advantage.

"Stoke your business, amp your life, and change the world—a modest promise, to be sure," she said with obvious understatement. "We'll take them one at a time, starting with business, okay?"

"That's what it's all about for me," Cam responded. "Chuck the other two, far as I'm concerned."

"Well, now that's just the problem, isn't it, Mr. Summerfield? You're not concerned far enough."

21.

In retrospect, I should have seen it coming, and if I'd known what was going on back at ILGI at that very moment, I'd probably have patted Cam on the head and said goodbye right then and there.

It's been called a lot of things throughout history: mutiny, uprising, revolt—insurgency is a popular one these days—but whatever colorful descriptor you choose, that's what was going down in the richly paneled office of Rich Delacroix.

He stood at the floor to ceiling window and looked down at the Mormon temple and at the highway beyond, wistfully picturing himself behind the wheel of his Mercedes Roadster. With the blue sky above and a V12 under the hood, he could rocket north toward San Francisco and soon be far away from the sudden, choking tension that had gathered in his office like a thunderhead. He could, that is, if it weren't for those three irritating letters that followed his name on the door: CEO.

Rich turned to face the six sales managers who comprised the entire team of Cam's direct reports. These were the folks responsible for the sales agents and Cam, in turn, was responsible for them, which, it should be obvious by now, was precisely the problem.

Lisa Appleman, a petite, crisply professional woman in her late twenties, spoke up first.

"There's a rumor going around the floor," she said, getting

right down to business, "that you're going to put Cam back on the phones, and that he won't be in management anymore, or something to that effect."

Rich sighed. Few things are more disconcerting than a leak in the executive team. He was going to have to figure out where the fissure was, but he couldn't think about that right now. Not with six pairs of eyebrows raised at him in anticipation. *Neither confirm nor deny*, Rich thought. He really hated politics but he also knew he had to handle this with more than a dollop of finesse. Whether they wanted him to or not, he certainly wasn't going to preside over a kangaroo court. Yet, these managers and their sales agents were the best in the business and the backbone of his company, so he damn well better listen to what they had to say on the contentious subject of Mr. Cameron Summerfield, SVP.

"Okay," said Rich. "Everybody have a seat and let's talk this through." They all sat on the sectional leather couches at the far end of the office and Rich continued.

"What have you heard, and what do you want to know?"

"First of all, is it true? Is Cam being demoted?" asked Sergio Velasquez, a manager who had been at ILGI about six months longer than Cam. He had watched Cam come on board, catch fire, and scorch right past him on the corporate highway. The day Cam became big boss man was the worst day of Sergio's professional life—not that he was one to hold a grudge or anything. "Because," he went on without waiting for an answer, "we think it would be better if you fired him altogether." Not that he held a grudge or anything.

"We?" exclaimed Lisa. "Speak for yourself, okay? That's insane. Cam's the best salesman any of us have ever seen. I'll take him on my team, Rich, and we'll kick your butt, Serge," she challenged with a grin.

"Fine, take him," said Sergio with a dismissive wave of his hand. "Just keep him and his smug, holier-than-thou attitude the hell away from me and my guys."

"Excuse me; may I say something?" said Rich with exaggerated calmness, a valiant attempt to overcome the pressure pulsating in his cranium. "What to do about Cam—if anything—is not your decision," his eyes moved back and forth between Lisa and Sergio. "It's mine. I do want to hear what you have to say, but the decision is ultimately mine and mine only. Everybody understand?"

All heads nodded, but only Sergio's tongue wagged. "Rich," he said with strained patience. "With all due respect, we're the ones who have to work with him day in and day out. We're the ones who have to clean up the messes he makes when he freaks out, intimidates, or even runs off someone on our team, and we're the ones who have to make sure that our agents are bringing in the numbers in spite of Cam's leadership, not because of it. So, of course you're the one who has to decide what to do, we get that, but there's something you need to get, too."

Rich stared at Sergio with raised eyebrows. "Which is?"

"If you make the wrong decision, you'll kill this management team."

22.

Agnes sat up and smoothed her sweater. "Let's start with the obvious: we're all businesspeople here, agreed? And can we all agree that we'd have no business without customers?"

We nodded.

"Okay; Business 101 completed, so let's move on. You boys better finish that cake, this is the one school where eating in class is required."

We obliged.

Agnes waved her hand. "I'm not going to rehash all the conventional customer service wisdom. If you don't know those things by now, then there's nothing I can do for you. Process is important; CRM technology, customer-focused strategies, complaint handling skills: all important. We can all get better at those things, to be sure. Right, sugar?"

"Yeah. I guess so, sure," said Cam, but without his trademark flippancy.

"But," she continued, "If you really want to stoke your business till it burns so bright that everyone will take notice, there are two things you must be with complete abandon." She paused and looked expectantly at each of us. "You may want to write these down."

That was obviously not just a friendly suggestion so I clicked the button on my pen.

"Hold on," Cam said. "That doesn't sound right. Don't you mean two things we have to *do*?"

"I most certainly do not," she replied firmly. "There are thousands of things to do, I'm not even going to pretend I know what they all are, but all those things will come from the two things to *be*. And they are," she forged ahead, "One: be deeply fascinated by the life of every person— customer, employee, colleague— your business touches; and two: be deeply grateful for who they are and what they do."

Cam squirmed but said nothing.

"Too flowery? Too girly? If there's one thing you should have gathered about me by now, boys, it's that I am certainly not made of sugar and molasses. I'll kick your ass from here to Hialeah if I think it'll help you, so don't you ever accuse me of being fluffy." She glared at Cam.

"I didn't say anything," he whined.

"Umm-hmm," she looked at him askance. "It all starts with the *heart*, Cam. If you develop a sincere love for people, you'll automatically be fascinated with and grateful for them. If you're fascinated with them, you'll discover how to add value to their lives. If you're genuinely grateful for their patronage, partnership, or friendship, you'll show them in ways that are sincere and meaningful. Those are the essential elements of a fabulously productive business relationship, or any relationship, for that matter."

This was familiar territory for me. "Pops called it 'do what you love in the service of people who love what you do.'"

She pointed to a small sign hanging on the wall behind the counter. I squinted at it, but the writing was too small for me to read.

"Pops and I kicked that around for years. He finally crafted the words just so, and it became his mantra. He taught it to anyone who cared enough to listen, which many did, of course, but there were only a few who really got it in their bones, you know? Edg has it, for example, and so does that lovely clown, Smitty. And maybe the both of you will, too." She zeroed in on Cam. "Is this making sense to you?"

"Whatever you say," he muttered.

"What?" I said, picking up his uneasiness with my refined sense of the obvious.

"This sounds like personal stuff, not business wisdom," he oozed.

"Well, baby," Agnes sighed, "contrary to what the old school bureaucrats would have you think, business is a deeply personal endeavor. Whether you intend to or not, you put your stamp on every bit of work you do, and you leave an indelible impression on every customer and colleague you touch. Each one of those impressions speaks volumes of truth about who you are. Business is not a mask; it doesn't hide your face. It unveils it, wrinkles, moles, warts, and all."

"I don't think so," said Cam starting, again, to fidget in his seat. "Work is work; personal is personal. Who I am at home and what I do there is nobody's business but my own."

"I'm not saying you should shower with your team, Cam," Agnes jabbed. "When you go to the bathroom, I'd much prefer that you close and lock the door, believe you me. Certainly, there are always lines of appropriateness, and each of us has to determine where to draw those lines. What is vital to understand, however, is that you can hide some of the things you do, but you can't hide who you are. And you shouldn't try to because your uniqueness is what sets you apart. I defy you to show me another Cam Summerfield anywhere on this planet."

God forbid, I thought to myself behind the bathroom door, as it were.

"That old saying, *it's not personal*; *it's business* is just plain false. Business is personal, personal, personal," she tapped three times on the linoleum tabletop for emphasis. "And," she twinkled, "is there anything in the human experience more personal than love?"

I regarded that as a rhetorical question.

"Love is your leverage," Agnes said. "And if you're observant, if you stay fascinated and grateful, love will hand you your competitive advantage on a solid gold platter." She rested her fingers on Cam's Wake-Up Pad. "This pad will only help you if you use it with your heart."

"Okay," huffed Cam. "Now we're getting a little too, like, *feel the force, Luke*. It's a *notebook*, Agnes, not a freakin' light saber."

"It's not magic, baby. There is, in fact, nothing more real and practical than applying love to the work you do."

"All right, then," Cam challenged. "Show me."

"I have been," she smiled, pointing to the front of the diner. "Since the minute you walked through those doors."

23.

"You fascinate me, Cam," Agnes cooed.

"Excuse me?"

"You heard me, *fascinate*. That's why I've been spending all this time with you. I love to discover things about people; and in that act of discovery I can oftentimes—not always, but often enough—figure out how to help. And if I can do that, I've earned a customer, a partner, or a treasured friend for life."

She turned to me. "And as Cam and I have more time together, which I certainly hope we will, I'll learn about him, about his life story, about the experiences that have made him what he is today. Doesn't that sound like a great deal of fun, Steve? Do you see how rich and rewarding that will be?"

Now it was my turn to squirm.

"What am I," said Cam with obvious discomfort, "a gorilla in the mist? What if I don't want to, as we say here in California, *share* any of that with you?"

"That's okay, sugar. I'll still learn about you by trying, but if you shut me out, that's your prerogative. Most people, though, will blossom under the attention. Let's take your sales department, for example."

"Yeah?"

"You're supposed to be their leader, right?"

"Supposed to be and am, yeah."

"All right then," she probed, "tell me one story about one accomplishment by one member of your team. Just one."

"All right, I will," he said trying to rise to her challenge. "Sue Proctor, a sales agent on this guy Sergio's team. She blew her quota away last month, after two consecutive months of probation. I didn't think she'd make it, but she did."

"How'd she do it?" I asked, not exactly fascinated, I admit, but certainly interested.

"Bottom line? She made a lot more calls and put in a bunch more hours. I think she worked on Sundays, too."

"You think?"

"No, I know. She worked on Sundays."

"That's it?" asked Agnes.

"What do you mean?"

"That's her story?"

"Yep."

"Tell me what you know about her."

"She's been working at ILGI for two years; before that she was a headhunter at a local boutique placement firm."

"That's not her story; that's her résumé," said Agnes. "Is that all you've got?"

"Look," Cam's voice rose slightly. "I don't have the time or the desire to…"

"Time is not the problem, Cam," Agnes cut in. "Desire is. You don't have it. You're not fascinated with Sue or, I'm guessing, anyone else in your department. True or false?"

Cam shook his head. "I'm deeply interested in their results, Agnes, that's my job. Once the results stop, so do I. We all say so long and that's that. Not everyone's cut out for this business, and if they're not, I'm not going to waste my time or the company's money coddling them."

"I agree with you, Cam, and I think Steve would, too." I nodded.

"But that's not the issue," Agnes said, lowering her voice to an emphatic whisper. "The problem is when your *superstars*' results suffer and they leave because of you— because they just can't stand working with you any longer. Or, just as bad, when people who could be superstars are never given the chance to blossom, to experience their own potential."

Harsh, but right on the money. That was the situation according to Rich, and it was precisely the reason he wanted me to work with Cam. I marveled at how Agnes was able to be so blunt without expressing the slightest hint of rancor. "You said earlier," she rolled along without giving Cam a chance to react, "that your demands of yourself and your team are identical, but they're not. You're fascinated with yourself; you know what makes you tick, you know your own dreams, hopes, and aspirations and you do what it takes to achieve those things, right?"

Cam crossed his arms and sat back confidently. "Of course, I do."

"And that's why you've broken all the sales records." He nodded. "Yes. I expect nothing less of myself."

"But getting *others* to break records is your job as a leader. In order to do that, you need to focus on *their* needs—*their* desires for *their* lives—and then show them how their performance at work will bring those things to fruition. You obviously don't, because you can't tell me one meaningful thing about any one of them. That's not only a lack of fascination on your part, baby; it's out-and-out contempt."

"Isn't that a bit much, Agnes?" I asked, surprised to find myself momentarily in Cam's corner. "That doesn't feel like contempt to me."

"Maybe not," she said. "But I'll guarantee you one thing."

"What's that?"

"It does to them."

24.

"I know what you mean, Agnes," I said, and then turned to Cam. "Let me give you a perfect example of what she's talking about."

The best Extreme Leader that I'd met in my years of doing this work was a midlevel vice president at a formidable national bank. When I first met him, Dick was running the check processing operation in the bank's corporate facility. It was the closest thing a bank has to a manufacturing operation and it had an ethnically diverse, primarily blue-collar employee base. Showing me around the facility, Dick beamed with pride and enthusiasm as he regaled me with story after story of unprecedented productivity increases and skyrocketing employee morale.

It occurred to me as we talked that Dick rarely used the pronoun, "I," as in, "I've done this; I've accomplished that." In fact, the word "we" didn't come up that often either; instead, he told me story after story about individual people and how they'd risen to conquer one enormous challenge after another—and he told many of those stories with the hero standing right there. Some appeared embarrassed by the spotlight, but every one of them, without exception, expressed some variation of a glowing "thank you" before scurrying back to work.

It's not as though Dick didn't have an ego. He could puff out his chest along with the best of them, but he saved that for the appropriate time, usually after dinner and more than a few drinks, and always tempered his boasting with a good shot or two of self-deprecation. Moreover, he always brought it back to one central theme: his deep gratitude for his employees' spunk, imagination, personalities, and drive. I remember getting the distinct impression that he was in awe of their accomplishments. In retrospect, I could see that he was, indeed—to use the word of the hour— fascinated with them.

Simply put, Dick loved the individuals on his team, even the ones he eventually had to let go.

Several years later, after his promotion to senior vice president—which was essentially deity status at the bank— surviving a merger, and moving to another division, Dick was charged with conducting what some euphemistically call a reduction in force. Over a twelve-month period, he culled his division from 1,500 people down to 175, mostly through outsourcing. During that same period, however, employee satisfaction percentages went from the mid seventies to the high eighties, raising steadily all throughout the process. That was counterintuitive. And it wasn't because the survivors were happy to still have a job— which they were— but anyone who's ever been through a layoff will tell you that the event is usually characterized by increased stress, cynicism, and even paranoia. That was not the case in Dick's domain.

When I asked him how he accounted for the amazing spirit and morale even as people were jetting out the door, he said, "Two things: I kept everyone involved and I continued to let them know I cared, every freakin' day."

Although, to be fair, being the potty mouth that he was, Dick's language was a bit earthier—a bit more colorful.

He didn't say freakin'.

Maybe that's part of the reason they loved him right back.

25.

"Your friend Dick is a storyteller," said Agnes, "because he loves the subject of his stories, and his desire to share their stories is how he shows his gratitude. More important, though, is that in learning their stories, he can adjust his approach and create the environment that will be the most productive for his team. That's the raw material for stoking your business."

"That guy didn't use a WUP, though, did he, Farber?" Cam allowed a small smile to cross his face.

"Never heard of it, I'm sure, Cam," I said. "But he'd have been all over it if he had." I was taking my own mental inventory of how much I really knew about my customers and colleagues, and I was coming up painfully short. I knew the basics, sure. After all, I had just told a story about Dick, but my knowledge of others didn't really run very deep at all. If Mary Ellen was able to do it on a glorified order pad, then I was sure I could, too.

"Well, then," Agnes said as she pushed herself up from the table. "That's a pretty good start for today, don't you think?"

"Start?" exclaimed Cam.

"Put it this way, sugar," she said as she looked around the diner. "Your fascination with others gives you the raw material to focus on and wrap your business around your customers and employees. Your gratitude keeps them engaged and coming back, but if that's all you do in your time on this earth, it will have been wasted time, to be sure. There are two more elements of the Radical Edge, remember?"

"Amp your life and change the world," I proclaimed, ever the alert student. Actually, I had written it in my WUP on one of the "Eavesdrop" pages, but given the situation, I didn't consider that cheating.

"Gotta have all three, boys. Gotta have all three." She turned to walk away and then paused and looked back at us. "By the way," she said as if she'd just remembered, "Your check has been taken care of by a friend of yours."

"Really? Who? Smitty?" I guessed.

"It doesn't really matter, does it, Steve? But be sure to show your gratitude to Mary Ellen with a nice, fat tip." She winked at Cam, and as she shuffled toward the front door she looked back over her shoulder one more time.

"See you tonight," she called. "And don't you dare be late." Tonight?

Tuning In

26.

This kind of thing shouldn't scare me anymore, but when I opened the door to my apartment and Smitty jumped out from the kitchen shouting an enthused *"Hey there, buddy!"* I nearly spat my heart right out of my mouth. *Definitely time to change the security code*, I thought as my eyes settled back in my head. He was drinking a glass of orange juice, which scared me, too, because I really couldn't remember buying it.

"Hope you brought that with you, Smitty, because if it came from my fridge, I can't vouch for its safety."

"Aged to perfection," he said, patting his stomach. "And guts of titanium."

"And to what do I owe this wonderful surprise? You get lost on your way to Nordstrom?" He was wearing a tie-dyed tank I figured had around the same purchase date as that orange juice.

"Just being the messenger, once again, my wry pal-o-meeno." He handed me a piece of paper with driving directions scrawled on it in thick pencil.

When Cam and I were leaving the diner, Mary Ellen had intercepted us and said she'd be calling me with directions to Agnes's house in Del Mar.

"Dinner is at six thirty," she said. "But Agnes usually turns in early, so don't plan on staying very long. And she drinks red, so you may want to bring a bottle of cab."

I don't know if Cam had mastered the look of incredulity before today, but he sure had it down now.

"I never said I was available for dinner," he'd said. "I've got plans tonight, so I'll have to pass."

Mary Ellen looked at me as if to say, *take care of it, please*, and hurried off to tend to a customer. So, I did. After cajoling Cam all the way back to the car, I'd finally gotten him to commit to one hour at Agnes's place. I'd closed the deal by offering to bring the wine, and we drove in blessed silence back to Mission Beach where he'd left his car last year—I mean earlier that morning.

"This is how Mary Ellen calls?" I said to Smitty. This guy was like a walking telegram. "Is this your new job, Western Union man?"

"I yam what I yam and I do what I do; if'n you don't like it then shame on you." He howled with laughter, having charmed the stuffing out of himself with his little rhyme. "So..." he wiggled his eyebrows above his tinted glasses, "how'd it go with little Cammie and Agnes the Magnificent?"

I wanted to say that I was hoping Cam would get stuck on the railroad tracks and run over by the Amtrak Coaster, but I was too nice to say that out loud. I didn't really mean it either, that would be way too troublesome for all those innocent passengers.

"We'll see about Cam," I told him. "Just when I think something is sinking into that concrete cranium of his he says or does something to really tweak my gizzards." I stopped for a moment, fished my WUP out of my shirt pocket, and wrote *tweak my gizzards*. I don't know why, just a spontaneous impulse, I guess. And I was trying to get myself in the habit of WUPing.

"But Agnes," I went on, "really is magnificent. I've never met anyone like her. I can't wait to spend more time just soaking up her perspective on things."

"Well, I sure wish I could be there with you for dinner at her house tonight," said Smitty. "I was invited, ya know," he insisted, catching my expression, "but I convinced her that it'd be better if I wasn't present and accounted for this evening."

"Why's that?"

"Just a feeling, that's all."

"What kind of feeling?" I asked with a subtle, growing sense of foreboding.

"Well, I think there's a storm comin' in, so I wanna be home where it's nice and cozy."

A storm in San Diego is newsworthy, but I hadn't heard anything about it and said so to Smitty.

"Not that kind of storm, you ninny."

"What do you mean? What other kind is there?" He shot me a roguish grin. "A shit storm."

27.

I drove the winding road up the cliff overlooking the deepening Pacific and took in the ridiculously beautiful view. The sun was heading down in the sky as I was driving up the road toward Agnes's house. I was more than a little curious about what kind of place I would find. Agnes struck me as simple and unpretentious, and I expected her house to be the same. I pictured a small, comfortable, one-story with a shingled roof and a neatly manicured wedge of grass out front. Maybe a little porch with a swing and a planter full of geraniums. That's why I soon found myself checking and rechecking the address on the page and comparing it with the plaque on the tall iron gate at the end of the street. There was no denying it, the number was the same, so I drove up and pressed the intercom button.

A moment later, the gate rolled aside and I eased up the driveway, lined on each side with enormous Canary Palms, the kind whose immense height and breadth and majestic quality always takes my breath away. If one of those massive fronds were ever to fall and hit you on the head, you'd be skewered to the earth like a shrimp on a spit.

I pulled into the driveway, paced up the steps to an oversized stained glass and hardwood door, and rang the bell, though I didn't need to. Before I could even take my finger off the button, the door swung open and Mary Ellen stood there, beaming.

And I mean beaming—as in radiant—as in hamma, hamma, hamma. She was dressed in a classy, black, designer evening gown with a string of black pearls swooping down her neck above a plunging V.

"Hamma, hamma, hamma," I actually said, ever the eloquent Casanova. "You look...you look..."

"Thank you," she laughed, mercifully letting me off the hook. "C'mon, follow me."

Not...a...problem. She took me down a hallway, which was like a celebrity photo gallery. Here was a young Agnes posing with the late, original Mayor Daley of Chicago machine notoriety; Agnes and the late Chicago columnist, Mike Royko, who was the perpetual thorn in Daley's side; Agnes with Oprah, with

Clinton, with Reagan, with Jim Belushi and Dan Ackroyd, with Jesse Jackson, and,—I almost passed out when I saw this one—a group shot with Agnes and every single scrawny and fantastic member of The Rolling Stones.

I dragged my chin along the floor down the hall and into the living room. The sun was settling down over the horizon and casting a red and orange glow on the surface of the sea. I knew this because I was looking at it through the panoramic window that arched around the round living room in which we now stood. The furniture was comfortable looking, very simple and classic so as not to attract attention to itself. Earth tones, greens, and muted purples created a warm, inviting environment that seemed to say, *come in, sit down, stay as long as you like.*

Ever the waitress, apparently, Mary Ellen took the two bottles of Silver Oak Cabernet that I'd brought and excused herself saying she still had some things to do in the kitchen. I walked up to the window and looked out at the breaking waves, way down at the bottom of the cliff.

"Do you like the view?" Agnes walked up behind me and put her hand on my back. I turned and gave her a hug and didn't bother to answer the question, not verbally, anyway. She gestured for me to follow her into a large but informal dining room, also with a spectacular view, and we sat down together at the table which was, I noticed, set for four.

"Cam should be here any second," I said after several minutes of my effusive praise for Agnes's amazing home. I nodded at the extra place. "Who else is joining us?"

The doorbell chimed and moments later Mary Ellen brought Cam in to join us at the table and then returned to the kitchen where we could hear her clinking dishes and clattering pans. We exchanged polite hellos and small talk until Mary Ellen emerged carrying four plates of endive and walnut salad in her experienced hands. The way she was dressed, she looked more like the lady of the house than the kitchen help, so I wasn't entirely surprised when she sat down and joined us at the table.

Cam did look a little startled, however.

"Mary Ellen is not only my treasured employee," Agnes explained, "but my caretaker here at home and," she rushed, not wanting to dwell on *caretaker*, "the cofounding director, with me, of the Foundation for Women in Social Enterprise."

Impressive, I thought. "But what about your kids?" I asked Mary Ellen, assuming that she lived here with Agnes. "I thought you were a single mom."

"I am," she said. "But the kids don't live with me."

"With their dad?" I assumed.

She laughed. "Not exactly. My son's thirty and my daughter's twenty-six, both out on their own and doing fine."

I gaped.

"I know," she said with a smile. "You don't have to say it. I look young. Good genes. But I make no secret of the fact that I'm fifty-one years old." She raised a glass of sparkling water in Cam's direction. "Old enough to be your mother."

He gave her a slow once-over. "Now, that would be a shame," he crooned.

A wave of nausea was not a good way for me to start dinner, so I hastily raised my wine glass in a toast and we all started in on our salads.

After a few mouthfuls, Cam gave an overly obvious gander at his watch and then looked impatiently in my direction as if to say, *better get this moving*. Not that I was all that eager to oblige him, but out of respect for Agnes's generosity with her time and wisdom, I tried to get the conversation started.

"So, Agnes," I said. "Is there a reason, other than sharing fine company and fabulous food, that you invited us here tonight?"

"Yeah, thank you," said Cam. "I don't mean to be rude, Agnes, but I do have to leave pretty soon. Is there a particular subject that you wanted to talk to us about?"

Maybe he really didn't mean to be rude—*maybe*—but he sounded like he was bracing himself for a classroom lecture from a billowing old windbag professor.

"Oh yes!" exclaimed Agnes. "The best subject of all, Cam."

"Okay. What is it?"

"You." She answered. "The subject on the table is you."

28.

"The second element of the Radical Edge is *amp your life*, remember?" she said, ignoring Cam's uneasy body language. "Have to have all three: business, life, and effect on the world, remember?" she asked again.

"Yeah, I remember," mumbled Cam.

"Well, if you're going to amplify your life, you'll have to first know who, exactly, you really are."

Agnes pushed herself up from the chair and walked over to a vintage looking radio perched on a shelf between the dining and living rooms. I had noticed it earlier with its oversized dials and jukebox era appearance. She clicked on the power and soft static hissed through the large grates of the radio's speaker.

"Hear that?" she asked.

"Just barely," I said. "But that's okay; it's just noise. You may want to adjust the antenna or the tuner..."

She cranked the volume up. "How about now?" she called. "It's louder, yes, but..."

She cranked again as if she were channeling the spirit of Mick Jagger from that picture on the wall.

"Now?" she was shouting over the noise.

The three of us at the table all clamped our hands over our ears and looked incredulously at each other. Leaving the tuning dial right where it was, Agnes mercifully turned the volume back down to barely audible fuzz and stood by the radio smiling as if she'd just shared with us a glorious composition.

"What's the matter?" she asked. "You didn't like that music?"

"That was noise," Cam groused.

"So it was," she admitted, bemused. "Well, then. Let's try that again."

Leaving the volume where it was, she now fiddled slightly with the tuning knob until the static evaporated and "Take Five" by Dave Brubeck jumped from a clear, crisp station. "Oh...a little jazz," Agnes delighted. "Louder, please," she said to herself and swung up the volume once again. This time, I noticed, none of us did any ear clasping whatsoever.

"Too loud?" she asked again.

"No, it's all right," I said. "That's one of my favorites, but I don't know how well I'm going to be able to hear everyone talk if you leave the volume where it is."

She nodded, turned the level down to where it filled up the background but didn't encroach on our voices, and came back to her chair. Silently, she placed her napkin back on her lap and reclined lazily, staring at Cam and then me.

She waited, saying nothing. Neither did I, or Mary Ellen, or Cam. Brubeck continued to swing in and out of the sound of the surf from the ocean below.

"Get the point?" asked Agnes.

Mary Ellen took a sip of wine and set her glass down. "That's one of her favorite demonstrations," she said with a smile. "Just think about it for a second. Loud static is annoying; loud music that you enjoy is exhilarating."

"And," Agnes broke in, "it's the same for each of us. The first thing we have to do is find our frequency, find our station, the one that clearly expresses who we are at our core. Have you ever," she turned to me, "helped your clients to find, clarify, and articulate their values or operating principles?"

"Sure. It's pretty standard procedure nowadays," I said, slipping easily into consultant mode. "Right up there with the vision thing."

"And it's important work, to be sure," she acknowledged. "But there's a missing piece, usually, in that process. Do you know what it is, Cam?"

"I know what they showed me when I started working, a poster on the wall with a bunch of statements about ILGI's values. That's all I know about it. I don't think it's any big deal one way or another." Again, he looked at his watch.

"That's a nice timepiece," commented Agnes. "May I see it? No...take it off and hand it to me, please."

Cam popped the clasp on his Tag Heuer and dangled the watch over the table. Agnes took it in her cupped hands and admired the workmanship. "Very, very nice," she cooed and handed it to Mary Ellen, who abruptly jumped to her feet and jetted into the kitchen, taking Cam's bling hostage. "Hey! What are you doing?" he cried as if she'd ripped off his pinky.

"Relax, sugar." Agnes patted his hand. "It's not going down the disposal; I'll give it back, I promise. I just don't like the competition.

"Now listen to me for two minutes, Cam." She laughed when he looked at his wrist and dropped his hand to his lap in frustration. "The core of your business is not your customer, it's not your product, it's not your numbers, it's not your company, and it's not your team. Do you know what it is?"

"I'll bet you're going to tell me, aren't you?"

She ignored the sarcasm. "It's you, Cam. You have no business, no money, and no *life* without yourself right at the center."

"That's obvious, Agnes."

"Yes, it should be. So answer me one simple, little question, baby, and I'll give you back your watch and let you go on your merry way. Fair enough?"

He nodded. "Sure. Okay."

"Who are you?"

He stared at her. "Is that a trick question?"

"Yes it is, but not in the way you think. The trick," she told him, "is not in how we answer the question; it's in our uncanny finesse in avoiding it altogether."

29.

"I already told you who I am, this afternoon at the diner," protested Cam.

"No. You told me what you've done. I'm asking you who you are." She paused for a moment and then relented. "Okay," she said. "We'll come back to you—if you want your watch back, that is."

Just then, Mary Ellen returned from the kitchen with four elegant plates of petite filets, small, perfect lobster tails, and lemon rice pilaf. She refilled our wine glasses, settled back in her chair, and placed her napkin on her lap.

"What did I miss?" she lilted, clearly knowing.

"I think you'll go first," said Agnes. "If you don't mind."

"I'm game," Mary Ellen laughed. "What am I going first with?"

"I think you're supposed to answer the who are you question," I said cutting into my steak. "And I'm pretty sure we don't want to hear your biography," I guessed.

"I'm all about service," she said without hesitation. "Everything I do comes from my desire to add more than I take from my relationships. Service fuels the way I work and the way I live my personal life, and it's the basis for all my choices. It's how I decide how I'm going to invest my precious time on this earth."

She'd obviously thought this through before, and I was impressed with her conviction and clarity in the way she delivered it.

Agnes said, "I made Mary Ellen my business partner because of the way she served our customers from the very first minute she started at The Wake-Up Call. And she cofounded the foundation with me for the same reason: she wanted to serve the needs of young women who, in turn, want to serve their communities. She served her marriage up until the minute her late husband—God rest his gentle soul—passed from cancer, and she still serves her children even though they're no longer living under the same roof."

"And," said Mary Ellen, looking at Agnes with gratitude in her eyes, "I serve my mentor here as her caretaker, though it doesn't really look like she needs one, does she?"

They raised their glasses to each other and sipped. It was a touching toast to deep camaraderie and friendship which couldn't possibly have gone unnoticed by our boy, Cam.

"So service is one of your core values," I said, trying to put it into a familiar language.

"If you like," said Mary Ellen. "But I prefer to think of it as," she pointed to the radio, "my frequency. It took me a while to find it, to tune in, as it were. There are a lot of values I hold dear: respect, integrity, honesty, love, and family, to name a few. But, for me, it all plays on the radio station called service." She clearly delighted in the metaphor. "Every value that I…well…*value* rolls up into service: service is the way I show respect; integrity and honesty characterize the kind of service I give to others. And if I'm really serving from my heart, I see everyone as family, not just my genetic relatives. That's the way it works for me, and the moment I got clear on that, the moment I tuned in, I committed to it with all my being."

"She turned up the volume," added Agnes.

"You amped your life," I said, catching the thread.

"And simultaneously stoked my business. Look at my career at the diner. I'm the *boss*, for goodness sakes!" she exclaimed with delight and a charming hint of self-deprecation. "And the foundation is one way I'm trying to change the world. I don't know how much of that I could have accomplished if I hadn't gotten clear on my frequency." Cam ate in silence, never taking his eyes off the plate.

I was enjoying Mary Ellen's dissertation immensely, but I couldn't wait for Cam's turn which, I suspected, was coming next. I admit that I was looking forward to hearing him confront such a personal revelation.

"Now," said Agnes, just as I'd hoped. "What about you?" I looked at Cam with near sadistic anticipation, practically licking my chops at the prospect of watching him try to tune in to his station.

"So?" she said again. "What about it, Steve?"

Cam's gaze shot suddenly up from his plate and over to me, and I felt myself recoil. First he looked surprised, then relieved, and then amused at this little turn of events.

Now who's the sadist? I mused.

"Okay, I think I can do this," I said, nervously rubbing my hands together. "I've done a lot of values clarification exercises with my clients over the years, and I think I've got it narrowed down to a few things that are really important to me, you know, values wise, but as far as my frequency, my one overriding value or principle goes, well, that I'm not too sure about, but I'll sure give it a try." I was blabbering.

"I'm, well, I'm a Capricorn, for starters." I laughed the worst kind of laugh, the kind where no one joins in. "Umm...okay... I...I value family too, just like Mary Ellen said. And integrity, of course, I mean, who doesn't, right?" They all looked at me while I verbally thrashed about. "But, really, I'm all about, well...*man*," I interrupted myself. "I'm surprised this is so hard."

"What's hard about it, sugar?" asked Agnes with genuine compassion for my predicament.

"Narrowing it down to just one thing; there's so much more to it than that. It reminds me of that character in the movie *City Slickers* who said the key was to find the one thing in your life. I always thought that was a little silly. Human beings are much more complicated than that."

"Yes, we are, but it's not about finding your frequency by ruling out everything else; on the contrary, it's about finding the frequency that includes all those other important values and ideals. The very act of trying to wrap it all together is what's really important because in order to do so, you have to get very clear on what you mean by each value and principle. You have to define them, think them through, understand them to their core, and evaluate your life against each one. The clearer you get, the closer you get to the frequency that pulsates through your life and characterizes who you really are. So, Steve, just try. Off the top of your head, now, answer me one question."

"Okay, I'll try,"

"What's most important to you in the way you live your life?"

"A lot of things are important," I said.

"Let's try that again," Agnes chuckled. "Say the first thing that comes to mind. What," she repeated, "is most important to you in the way you live your life?"

"Freedom," I said, almost without thinking. "For me, I guess, it's all about freedom."

I'd never thought about it that way before, and the word surprised me. What was most shocking about it, though, wasn't the spontaneity of my utterance, and it wasn't the forceful way the word flew out of my mouth. It was the joy I felt in the act of saying it.

And the sudden comprehension that it was true.

30.

"Well," said Agnes. "That sounds just lovely. *Freedom*. Now what does that mean, Steve? Can you make that clearer for us? Can you turn it up a bit?"

"It's what I've always wanted for myself, I guess, and for others."

"In what way?" coaxed Mary Ellen.

"The freedom to say what I think. The freedom to spend my time doing the things that bring me joy. Freedom of creative expression, the freedom to love without judgment. I think that's accurate." I was thinking out loud. Freely, I might add. "I think that's why I'm pulled to the field of leadership development, to help others experience that sense of freedom that comes from accomplishing extraordinary things in life. I mean, unleashing the potential in others is really the act of liberation, isn't it? Freeing the human spirit?"

"Makes sense to me," said Mary Ellen, and Agnes nodded in agreement.

"Yeah," I admitted. "Makes sense to me, too."

"That's a terrific start, baby," encouraged Agnes. "Now, here's what I want you to do." She leaned forward, and so did I. "Where's your WUP?"

"My WUP?" I said, patting my pants pockets.

"Don't tell me you don't have one. I know you left the diner with my order pad, Steve," said Mary Ellen. "I saw you take it." She wagged her finger at me. "I don't miss much, you know."

A wave of guilt settled over my head like a soft cloud. "I left it at home, I think. I didn't know there was going to be a quiz."

My intention was not to be funny, but it sure got a guffaw out of Cam. "Yeah, neither did I," he said. I guess he didn't bring his, either.

"There's always a quiz," corrected Agnes in all seriousness. "That's why you have to carry it with you all the time. I want you to write freedom in your WUP the second you get home, and then spend at least thirty minutes writing down what the word means to you."

"And then do what I did when I first tuned in to service," added Mary Ellen. "Start to list all the ways you can think of to bring more freedom into your life and the lives of others. And then, if freedom really is your frequency, as you do more of those things, your energy will kick up to levels that you've never experienced before."

"And if it isn't the right one?"

"Start over," she said. "And keep going until you find the one that is."

"It could take a while," said Agnes. "From the time I was a little girl in Chicago, I knew I wanted to have a restaurant. I was positively in love with the idea. I went to med school to please my parents, but I could never shake the fantasy. When I finally opened my first Agnes's Real Chicago Hot Dog and Chili Palace, I thought I'd arrived. But it wasn't until a few years later when I was about your age, young Mr. Cam, that I finally got clear on and tuned into who I really was beyond the labels of chef, or entrepreneur."

"And who was that?" I asked.

"I was and am and evermore will be devoted to human growth. When I realized that, I devoted more and more time and energy to the education and development of each and every one of my employees. Now these were fry cooks, mind you: cooks and cashiers and sweepers and cleaners who all started at the minimum wage, but I sought out opportunities for them to take on more challenge and responsibility. My business started to grow as well, and my employees took management jobs in my new locations. They became businesspeople in their own right, and some went on to start places of their own.

"Everything I do—*everything*—is with the intention to bring out the full capacity of those around me. And that's how I continue to grow, too, and will until the day I shuffle off to that Hot Dog Palace in the sky."

"I'm only one of many examples of what Agnes is talking about," Mary Ellen said, resting her hand on Agnes's shoulder. "I am living evidence that this woman's growth frequency is not only crystal clear; her volume is turned all the way up to ten."

"So amping your life on the growth frequency helped you to stoke your business, as well," I commented.

"And change the world. Don't forget about that, baby. But we'll get to that."

Cam cleared his throat and all heads swiveled to him. "Dinner was great; I wish I could stay for dessert, but," he tapped his naked wrist. "I gotta bolt. I'm sure you don't need to pawn my watch, ladies, so if I could have it back, please, I'll get out of your way and you all can continue with...ah...*group*, or whatever you call it."

"Not until you've earned it," Agnes sang. "A deal's a deal, sugar. I believe it's your turn to answer the question."

"You mean, who am I?"

"That's the one," I said, relieved that the focus had shifted to Cam.

"My name is Cam Summerfield. My rank is senior vice president. My employee number is 135. My *frequency* is impatience and my time is now up. Watch, please." He held out his hand.

I'm a pretty laid back, find-the-humor-in-the-situation kind of a guy. Most folks will tell you that I'm easygoing, quick to forgive, and slow to anger. But the people who know me well—my family, some close friends, for example—know something about me that others do not: I have a low aggravation threshold. When that threshold is crossed; when the dam is breached, if you prefer, it's not a pretty sight. I have been known to blow like Moby, and, although I don't see what the big deal is, I've been told that I scare the living hell out of those on the receiving end. Cam did not know this about me, nor did anyone else in our little dinner party. My new little buddy of the day, however, was dangerously close to igniting my inner Hulk. I felt a familiar, David Banner-like tremor building somewhere deep in my chest.

I think Agnes must have sensed something because she asked Mary Ellen to retrieve the watch and told Cam that she understood, and that it was just fine, sugar, it was a pleasure to have his company if even for a short while. It was hard to hear through the thunder raging in my ears, but that was the gist of it.

I breathed, took another breath, and said, "Just one moment, please."

Then I waited for Mary Ellen to sit back down before I continued. "Cam, if you've listened *at all* to *anything* that these wonderful women have shared with us this evening," I was really trying not to hiss, "then you know that they didn't invite us here for their own good. They're doing just fine, thank you very much."

So far, so calm. I paused for a gulp of water.

"Now, I've learned a lot tonight, and I'm very grateful for that," I felt myself calming a little. Gratitude will do that to you. "But we're here for your benefit, Cam. Don't you get that? They invited us here to help you, and I think it would be the honorable, right thing for you to try, at least. "So," I spoke into his silence, "how about really trying to answer the question, okay? Cam? Would you do that, please?"

"Okay," he started sweetly enough, "How about this? How about it's none of your flippin' business who I am or what my *freeeeeeequency* is." He made his voice warble like *The Outer Limits*. "I've answered the damn question. I'm a moneymaker. I'm a hard worker. I've earned my stripes and that's all you need to know. You wanna know my story? Fine. Here it is: I grew up poor. When I was little, I slept in a drawer in my mother's bedroom. I fought my way through high school and swept floors at the 7-Eleven for money because I never had an allowance. Is that what you want to know? Boo-hoo, poor me. Is that what you want to hear?

"You wanna know my frequency, Agnes?" he snarled. "It's get mine. That's it. Nobody's gonna give it to me, so I'm going to get it myself. Okay, now?" he shouted. "Everybody happy? Is that *amped* enough for you?"

"Enough!" I shouted back. "You don't get it, do you, you ungrateful, self-centered little punk? Because of you, I got the chance to meet and learn from these remarkable people, and I'm glad for that, but you, Cam, are not worth another nanosecond of effort from me or anyone else. That's…that's it for me; I'm done with you. I'll call Rich in the morning and tell him you're on your own. And good *flippin'* luck to you."

I got up and left to find the bathroom. I closed the door behind me and rested my forehead against it. I turned on the tap in the sink, splashed cold water on my face, and looked at myself in the mirror. Already the waves of regret and failure were rolling over me.

Here I was, supposed to be a leadership coach, but I couldn't find it in myself to work with this kid who undoubtedly needed help more than anyone I'd ever worked with before. What could

I do, though? He didn't want it or he was just too proud to admit that he did. Either way, I had to let it go and chalk it up to experience. Maybe this failure would make me a better coach for others that I'd meet down the road.

What had I learned from this? That's another question to work out on my WUP, I figured. I dried my face on a soft, cotton towel embroidered with small, purple flowers, took a few more deep breaths, and headed back to the dining room.

Cam was gone, and Mary Ellen was clearing the table in silence.

"Feel better?" Agnes asked with a knitted brow.

"Well, that's that," I sighed as I sat and poured myself a cup of dark, rich coffee. "I really botched that one all to hell, didn't I?"

"If it makes you feel any better, baby," she said, "he did thank us for dinner before he left." Her laughter that followed did make me feel better.

The three of us moved to the living room and sat facing each other in soft, upholstered brown and green loveseats. I set my cup down on the coffee table and leaned back into the comforting little sofa. "I'm really sorry, ladies," I said. "That was totally unprofessional and uncalled for. I wish I could call a do-over."

"Don't worry about it, Steve," said Mary Ellen on behalf of the both of them. "We all lose it from time to time. I know I have."

"Oh, yes," agreed Agnes. "My blowouts make yours look like a delicate spring shower." They both had a good laugh at that from a shared history, no doubt.

"I was really impatient with him all day, you know? Tonight pushed me over the edge, but I was already teetering on it. What else could I have done?" I pleaded.

"Why are you so worried about it, sugar?"

"Isn't it obvious?" I said. "I'm supposed to help people like Cam, not chase them away."

"The modern malady, Steve, is people living lives of quiet desperation. The three of us here, and many others like us, the ones who want to use their gifts to change the world for the better, prefer to live lives of amplified exuberance. That's how we move mountains, baby. Cam isn't ready to look deep enough into himself to find that clear, inspiring voice. So, even though it's in there somewhere, he's got nothing to amplify. Not yet, anyway."

"Besides, what makes you think you didn't?" asked Mary Ellen.

"Didn't what?"

"Help him."

"Were we all at the same dinner?" I looked at each of them. "That was a complete, total, and utterly miserable failure."

They each looked at me. "Wasn't it?" I said.

"No, baby, it wasn't," said Agnes the Wise. "You helped him more than you know. We all did."

The Reunion

31.

I drove back to my apartment in silence. That may not sound strange given that I was by myself, but usually I've got the music cranked up—a little Stevie Ray or John Hiatt, maybe—and I'm yowling along like an auditioning *American Idol* contestant. I was thinking about Cam, of course, and trying to come to terms with the whole deal. Who knows? Maybe there was still hope for him.

As I crossed over the bridge to Mission Beach and saw the roller coaster lit up in all its urban glory, my thoughts, for some reason, turned to my daughter, Angelica. She was just about Cam's age, I realized with a start. When she was younger she, too, was leading a life of quiet desperation, as do many young teenagers who haven't yet discovered their own frequency.

In some ways, my daughter was different from her peers. Instead of fighting to get out of the house, as most teenagers do, Angelica preferred to stay in the family nest and take care of her younger brothers. At fourteen, she was a domestic, maternal, and altogether lovely child—and, I have to admit, it was great having a built-in babysitter under the same roof. As she approached her seventeenth birthday, however, she was still a homebody.

I know that many parents would kill to have their teenagers stay at home, but what troubled her mother and me was *why* Angelica stayed home. She was a paradox of confidence: at home she was queen of the roost and a paragon of responsibility to her brothers. Away from home, however, she was fearful as a finch outside its cage. We came to realize that we had far more confidence in Angelica's abilities than she had in her own, and that we needed to create a situation where Angelica could prove herself to herself.

So in the summer of Angelica's seventeenth year, we sent her away—far away. We sent her to Italy, by herself, for six weeks. On one level, she desperately wanted to take this trip; on another, she was terrified.

We found her a room in Florence and enrolled her in Italian language and fine art classes. Before she left, Angelica and her mother planned every minute of her travel schedule down to the finest detail: she would fly from San Francisco to New York's Kennedy airport, switch planes, and fly on to Milan. At the Milan airport she would catch a bus to the station in central Milan, get on a train, and ride another seven hours to her cousin's house. She would stay there and decompress for a few days before traveling up to Florence where her Italian living and studying adventure would finally begin.

You may think it extreme of us to send our daughter on such a potentially perilous journey. You'd be right in the conventional, suburban sense, I suppose, but we knew she could handle it. She only suspected she could.

On the day of her departure, watching her walk down the Jetway at SFO, I had a vicarious jolt of joy and liberation. I remembered the first time I'd gotten away from my father and set out on my own. "She's going to have the time of her life," I whispered to her mother. Before she stepped through the airplane door, Angelica turned and, with a tremulous half smile on her face, waved goodbye. *She's going to have the time of her life*, I said to myself.

I didn't fully realize, however, that I would never see the same little girl again.

Several hours later, Angelica arrived in New York and, embracing the power of the phone card—remember those from the pre-cell days?—called home.

"I'm in New York and you didn't tell me I was going to have to switch terminals.—I had to take a bus!—and the flight to Milan is delayed and I'm at the gate and I'm okay and *I'm ready to come home now!*"

We calmed her down and reassured her that she really was okay, and that everything would be fine as soon as she got on the plane. The flight was delayed for five hours—we got the hourly update—and we gratefully breathed a sigh of relief when Angelica was finally winging her way to Milan. She landed several hours later, got off the plane and went directly to the nearest phone.

"I'm in Italy now and I'm going to catch the bus and I couldn't figure out how to use the phone and I think I know where the bus is and *I'm ready to come home now!*"

Again, we calmed her down. She found the bus, took it to the train station and again, one hour later, she called home:

"I'm at the train station now!"

Her mother and I, standing in our kitchen back in Marin County, California, felt like we were in the war room, like we should be moving a pin on a giant wall map and shouting *she's made it to the train station!* into the radio.

"And the schedules are different from what we thought and nobody speaks English and I found the right platform and *I'm ready to come home now!*"

I'm not exaggerating; I am quoting verbatim. We calmed her once again and seven hours later, from her cousin's house, guess what? She called.

"Now, *look*," she said to her mother. "I made it to New York, I made it to Milan, I made it to the train, and now I'm here. *And now I am ready to come home.*"

So I got on the phone and I said to her, "Listen, honey, I gotta tell you something: You're having the time of your life. You just don't know it yet."

To say that the person who came home six weeks later had had the time of her life would be a gross understatement. What she'd done, in fact, was created a new life entirely.

The next summer Angelica backpacked around Europe, and the summer after that she and her mother volunteered in a Guatemalan orphanage. She did her junior year of college in Madrid, Spain, and years later, when she was twenty-three, she took a summer internship with the US State Department at the American consulate in—who says life is random—Milan.

She was one of four interns accepted out of five thousand applicants. And even though the Foreign Service was not, she was to discover, her cup of tea, she is now a bona fide woman of the world with a global perspective on life and the human condition.

To this day, I feel great about having helped her to discover more of her own capability. The truth of the matter is, though, all I did was give her a nudge, a nudge that she would have fought with her every fiber if she hadn't wanted it in the first place.

Cam was going to stay right where he was, I figured, because he didn't want it any other way.

Mission Boulevard was teeming with pedestrian traffic as I turned onto my street and pulled around back to the garage. I clicked the door opener and pulled in. The garage had been empty when I left, it always is, but there was something sitting right in the middle of the floor. I slammed on the brakes and jumped out to take a look.

It was a skateboard, and it wasn't mine, I knew, because I've never owned one. I always figured that it would be a lot easier simply to smash my knees with a sledgehammer. I picked it up and gave one of the scuffed wheels a spin. The decal on the underside of the board was a cartoon of a skateboarder doing a handstand of sorts. His right hand was planted on the ground and his left held the skateboard to his feet, which were sticking up in the air. The trick was called a handplant, and I'd always enjoyed watching skaters who could pull it off. Two things made this picture different, however: he was handplanting on the edge of a steep cliff and, scarier yet, he was wearing a suit and tie.

I tucked the board under my arm and walked up the back stairs to the patio outside the kitchen, fished for my key, and opened the door. I made a quick call to Rich Delacroix's office and left him a message that we needed to talk first thing in the morning. I didn't want to leave the gory details on his voice mail and, more important, I wasn't yet sure what, exactly, I was going to tell him.

I walked into the living room and kicked off my shoes. Mary Ellen's pad, my WUP, lay on the end table where I'd left it, but it looked different.

Someone had doodled in it.

32.

I tore into my WUP that night, trying to capture as much as I could of what I'd learned from that evening's discussions and events. I wrote my freedom list; I scribbled some thoughts about Cam and Agnes and Mary Ellen. I just let it roll, trying not to judge my observations, as per Smitty's explicit instructions. Several hours later, still reflecting on my daughter's Italy experience, I called and left a goodnight message on Angelica's cell phone, bolted all the doors from the inside, for obvious reasons, and threw myself into bed.

Falling asleep is usually the least of my challenges, but that night I tossed like the surf had rolled up under my bed. I chalked up the skateboard and WUP doodles to Smitty's eccentric glee in invading my apartment, so that didn't bother me too much. The day's conversations and the blowup with Cam, however, gave me a lot to think about, and my mind just wouldn't stop boiling. The morning couldn't come soon enough.

I didn't need the alarm, but I waited for it anyway. I jumped up, showered, dressed, scooped up the skateboard, and drove down to the address in Ocean Beach that Agnes had given me before I'd left her house.

There was going to be a meeting, she'd told me, that I wouldn't want to miss. "A network of extraordinary people," she'd said, who get together once a month to encourage, inspire, and cajole each other to *keep on keepin' on*, as we geezers used to say. A skate park seemed like an odd place for that kind of meeting, but that's where the address led me.

The sign over the small building said *SKATE!* in all caps and italics. I pushed through the doors and walked up to the counter. The back of the room had a giant arched doorway leading out to a large outdoor lot built up with a series of concrete and wooden ramps, rails, stairs, and small empty swimming pools. Large block letters etched on the archway formed two words that I could only assume expressed the personality and purpose of the establishment and its extreme customers:

NO POSERS

There were a couple of skaters crisscrossing each other on a giant half-pipe, a large, U-shaped ramp popular with the more accomplished skaters. I could hear the gravelly grind of wheels. They made no sounds, whoops, or yelps at all as the skaters focused to master their stunts.

I walked through the archway to get a closer look—I love to watch that stuff—but a young man with a hoop in his nose and a pin through his lip stopped me in my tracks. He wore a T-shirt with a complex, colorful pattern of dragons and knights coiled up together like intricate, braided strands.

"'Scuse me, sir," he said gently. "Are you Mr. Farber?"

"I am," I said. "But you can drop the Mr." The label makes me shudder, especially since the second I turned forty. "Farber or Steve will do just fine," I reached out my hand and he took it in a firm grip.

"Well you can call me Mr. Garcia, then," he laughed. "Agnes asked me to watch for you and bring you back to the meeting room. C'mon with me. Everyone's already here. There's plenty of coffee and some munchies back there, if you're interested."

"Always," I said and followed him through a door on the left side of the counter and into a large, modest room set with card tables and folding chairs. The seating was arranged in a large square so everyone could see each other. There were twenty-five, maybe thirty, people already sitting and listening intently to one of their peers. A few heads turned toward the door as we walked in and a man in a crisp blue suit and crimson tie motioned me over to the seat on his left.

"Thanks, Mr. Garcia," I whispered to my escort, for some reason expecting that he'd be leaving, but he sat down in an empty chair and shuffled through a notebook on the table in front of him. I walked over, sat down next to Mr. Brooks Brothers, and took a quick inventory of the faces around the room.

There was no consistent theme or pattern here. Agnes, whom I saw as soon as I came in, was by far the oldest of the gaggle, and the good-natured Mr. Garcia—I'd put him at eighteen or nineteen—was clearly the youngest. Black, white, Asian, Hispanic, Indian, male and female, young and old, sharp clothing, shorts, and sweats—this crowd was a diverse and lively mix of people who were clearly engaged and happy to be in the same room together. I was suddenly aware that a silence had settled over the gathering.

"Steve?" Agnes was asking, apparently for the second time, at least.

"Oh, I'm sorry," I said. "Hi, Agnes, everybody." I did a little embarrassed wave around the room.

"Glad you could join us," said Agnes. "I asked you to come a little bit late so I could tell the group about you before you got here, which I've already done."

Several people nodded and smiled; a few mouthed hi, hello, good morning, and the like. "I'm afraid I'm at a bit of a disadvantage, folks." I talk to groups for a living, so I'm perfectly comfortable having all eyes on me. Some would even say I prefer it.

However, usually I know why I'm talking in the first place. "I'm not really sure what's...what's going on here."

Several sympathy laughs broke out around the room. I always take that as an encouraging signal. "That didn't come out right. What I mean is, Agnes told me a little about how some folks get together to support each other and all that. That's pretty much all I know. So...Agnes?"

"So...Steve?" She was playing with me.

"Mind telling me what happens now?"

"Certainly, baby, happy to. Now you get to hear from the experts about the third element of the Radical Edge. You know what I'm talkin' about."

"Yes, I do. Change the world."

"Now that," Agnes laughed, "is a mighty fine idea."

33.

I've always wondered what it would be like to be the surprise guest on a game show like *This Is Your Life*, or to be the focus of *Extreme Makeover: Personality Edition*. Now, with the way all these people were looking at me, I had an inkling. It wasn't exactly comfortable.

"But why, if I may ask, all the attention on me? I can't possibly be the purpose of your meeting, and, well, a little context would be helpful here, I guess."

"If I may," cut in Mr. Brothers with a voice as refined as his suit. "You *are* the center of attention this morning, Steve."

"I are?"

"Yes, just as everyone in this room was in the very beginning."

"I'm sorry, the very beginning of what?" This might have been creepy if these people hadn't seemed so nice.

"All of us here," he explained, "have devoted ourselves, personally and professionally, to changing the world, in some way, for the better. We all strive to use what we have—talent, desire, resources, imagination, time—to make a difference, if I may use the cliché. To put it another way, to expand the *rightness* of things.

"We don't consider ourselves to be naïve or idealistic, although others certainly may. We are pragmatists of the highest order. We believe there is nothing more eminently practical than looking at the world, asking how can this be better? And then holding ourselves personally accountable for getting it done.

"So, what we have here, Steve, is a collection of businesspeople—some independent owners, some corporate executives, some employees, some social entrepreneurs— who all have one common desire: to help each other to help each other."

I let that settle for a moment as I looked around the room for any signs of dissonance or cynicism. I saw none, so I gathered that this sharp-dressed dude was doing a good job as spokesperson.

"What we also have here, Steve," he continued after a short pause, "is an invitation. We are inviting you to join us."

"Come again?" I said.

"Agnes gave us your background this morning. She told us a lot about you. Not everything, I'm sure, but enough for us to know that you would benefit from us," he gestured to the group, "and we, from you. If you'd care to, that is."

"Well, I'm honored, I think. But I'm not so sure what I have to bring to the...um...tables."

"I think you have a lot," Agnes chimed in. "But let us tell you what we're all about, and then you can decide. Is that fair?"

I nodded. "Sure."

"By the way," said the Suit. "I'm Ronald Perricone. I'm an executive at Maritime and Son."

My head snapped around to take him in again in a new, surprising light.

"This group, gathering, network—whatever you choose to call it—was founded many years ago by William Maritime and Agnes Golden. It started with the two of them at Agnes's diner and expanded over the years from a duo to this group that you see here today, all through personal invitation."

"Invitation based on what? How do you decide who gets to sit in the position I'm in right now?" I was also wondering about initiation or hazing rites, but I kept that to myself.

"There are no specific criteria, Steve. We don't try to quantify the kind of colleague we want; instead, we look for someone whose intent to change the world is as deep as ours is. People tend to group with others who are most like themselves, and we don't want to homogenize."

My mind flashed back to the team of Jims.

"The only similarities we look for are intent and conviction. We are interested in those who strive—and that's an important word— to change a piece of their world for the better. We're not interested in talkers; only practitioners. And there's one more critical factor."

"What's that?" I asked.

"Let me put it this way: when we get together it feels much more like a reunion than a work session. We love each other's company; therefore, we only invite people whom we're pretty sure we're going to love."

"Well...then I'm honored, I guess. I'm a loveable guy, that's true," I mugged. "But I don't know if I qualify as a practitioner."

"We think you're underestimating yourself, but let me finish telling you what we do here. Once a month we get together and compare notes about what we're seeing in the world around us and what we're trying to do in response to it."

That's when I noticed that each person around the tables had some kind of notebook, pad, or electronic gadget placed on the table in front of them. Some were yellow legal pads, others were spiral or steno books, and a few electronic tablets and assorted laptops were glowing up at their owners. They were all variations, I gathered, of the same species: they were all WUPs.

"And then," Ronald continued, "we try to come up with some solutions, some new ideas, and some breakthroughs for one another—"

"—in order to change things for the better," I added.

"Exactly," said Ronald. "And at the same time add more value to our respective businesses and bring more joy to our lives.

"Changing the world is our ultimate responsibility as Extreme Leaders, but not at the expense of the other aspects of our lives. In other words, we change the world using the vehicle of business and the instrument of our individual uniqueness."

"We're tuned in to our own frequencies," Agnes winked, making a knob turning motion with her right hand. "And we're using them to change the world. Nothing more personally thrilling and rewarding than that, now, is there?" I took out my WUP and noticed several smiles and nods of approval.

"Good!" encouraged Ronald. "There are four change-the-world guidelines that we've agreed on so far, but we're always open to more, and I'm sure we're missing more than a few things. Let me spell them out for you."

I wrote a heading and date on the top of the page. "The first is to define what you mean by world, and get clear on how you want that world to be different from the current reality. World doesn't have to mean the very fabric of human existence, although it certainly could be. It could be the world of your customers, neighborhood, industry or the world of one person, for that matter. You define it for yourself.

"For example, Stan over there is the CEO of an assisted-living company devoted to changing the world of senior care. When he first joined us, Stan said this: 'When a person's biggest risk is trying to get through the day without falling down, that's not a great life.' So, Stan and his team create an environment at his facilities where people in their seventies, eighties, and nineties are encouraged to take on challenges and risks. Stan is proving to his own customers that they're still capable of living lives of great adventure and meaning, and he's proving to the rest of his industry that there's a better way to do things. And, by the way, he comes down here from Vancouver every month to join us."

Ronald went around the table and gave a quick overview of the members and their businesses. Some focused on the world of their employees, and others on the world of their particular industry and some, like my friend, Mr. Garcia, on his own neighborhood.

"Raul Garcia, over there," Ron pointed at him with a smile, "has a silk-screening shop in Mission Beach and probably sells more T-shirts than anyone along the boardwalk. He's the best salesperson you're ever going find, I'll wager. His enthusiasm is contagious, and there's no way you can walk into his shop without buying at least one shirt, and don't be surprised if you walk out with a closetful."

"One correction," said Raul. "No one who buys a shirt will ever leave with just one."

"That's pretty confident," I challenged.

"No, it's a fact," he countered. "You wanna know why?"

"You betcha," I said.

"Because if they buy one, I'm gonna give 'em another, whether they want it or not. I don't advertise that. I want my customers to advertise it for me. I want them to go home and say, *you gotta check this place out.*"

I was impressed with this young dude who obviously had *merchant* stamped all over his DNA, but I had to ask one question:

"That's very cool, Raul. But how, exactly, does that change the world?"

"It doesn't," he said. "But I got a hell of a business going, don't I?"

Everyone laughed, including me, but I knew there had to be more to it.

"Seriously, though, dude," Raul said. "I'm changing the world of my neighborhood by the way I hire my employees who are, by the way, the best salespeople in the world, next to me."

"How's that?" I asked.

"They're all homeless street kids when I first get a hold of 'em. Do you have any idea what kind of will and smarts it takes to survive on the street? I find kids with personality and drive, and I nurture it. I figure if I can channel some of that into something productive—" His voice trailed off for a moment and then picked up steam again. "Sometimes I get screwed, taken advantage of, ripped off, even, but that's the price I pay to find the ones that pay off for themselves and for me. The street is filled with unbelievable talent. I know it firsthand."

"Because?"

"Because that's where I came from, dude. Lived on the streets from the time I was eleven years old until the day someone gave me an opportunity: the guy that started the shop; the guy that retired and sold it to me on my eighteenth birthday; the guy that changed my world. Now that's the way I do it, too."

"Wow."

Not profound, I know, but there was really nothing else I could say.

34.

There was no doubt that I was in the presence of greatness, but it was—how can I put this—*normal* greatness. These were not extraordinary, saintlike people. They were just totally committed to making a positive mark on the world, and, from what I could tell, they were all doing very well in their businesses. At least they felt they were. And unless you're a publicly traded company, that's good enough in my book. Even so, I knew we were just scratching the surface.

"Second guideline is," Ronald said, "act as though your every action has a direct impact on the world. In other words, you should perform every deed as if it will either improve the world or damage it."

"But, that's not true," I argued.

"I didn't say it was. I said act as though it were. There's no downside to that, is there? It gives us the mindset that we need to keep trying, whether anyone else is watching or not. Personal—even radical—accountability is when you do what it takes to change the world regardless of what anyone else is or isn't doing."

"That seems like an impossibly high standard," I said.

"If I may," said Agnes. "It is a high standard that we may or may not be able to live up to. Nevertheless, it's also our way of reminding ourselves that none of us is isolated; none of us lives in a vacuum. And that is the truth. You can't deny this reality, sweetheart, the world already changes because of your influence. Each person you touch, each comment you make, each action you take hits a button, strikes a chord in someone else, gets them to think a thought or do something—no matter how small—that they wouldn't have done or thought if you hadn't connected with them. You have no idea how far that influence goes. It may last a split second or it may take them on an entirely new course. It may be good; it may be bad. It may be nothing more significant than the flutter of an eyelash or a fleeting feeling. But you cause *something* to happen, and that's the Lord's honest truth."

"You're not talking about the butterfly effect, are you?" I've always been leery of the loose way people tend to use the principle.

"You mean because you pick your nose in Singapore someone hits the lotto in Poughkeepsie?" asked Agnes with forced seriousness.

"That's the oversimplified way folks talk about it, yeah," I laughed.

"Oh my, who knows, baby? That's way beyond me, and that's for certain. All I'm saying is you're not alone on this planet no matter how isolated you may feel at times. So, instead, try to act like you're connected because—well, because you are."

Ronald picked up the thread from there: "Maybe your actions won't even be a blip on the cosmic radar screen, but so what? At least you'll have lived your life trying, and that's the only thing any of us has any control over; which brings us, conveniently, to the third guideline."

"Gimme one second, please," I said as I scratched some hasty notes in my WUP.

Ronald waited, checked to make sure I was ready, and then forged ahead.

"Third," he said. "Don't judge yourself based on the outcome of your efforts."

"Meaning?"

"Meaning you cannot ultimately control the end results. You do everything you can, you do your homework and your research, and you enlist the people you need to get the job done, whatever it is. Whether it's senior care, selling T-shirts, or coaching people to be better leaders, whatever it is you're trying to do. You define world, you get clear on how you want that world to change, you act as though all of your actions will make it happen, and then...then sometimes you succeed and sometimes you bomb, or maybe it's somewhere in between, but in any case, you never, ever judge yourself based on the outcome. If you succeed, you don't take credit for it; if you fail, you don't blame yourself. The only thing you take credit for is the fact that you tried."

I flashed back to last night's fiasco at Agnes's house. I'd wanted desperately to take credit for a miraculous transformation in the life of Cam Summerfield, I now saw. Moreover, I blamed myself for not making it happen. *I have a little work to do on guideline number three*, I thought.

"Like I said before, these are just guidelines, and there are, we're sure, a lot more where they came from. They're simple in concept and remarkably hard to practice, but that's what we're doing, practicing."

"But you said there were four," I remembered. "What's the last one?"

"Never—never, *ever*—" he resonated, "try to do it alone."

35.

Just then, the door flew open and banged against the wall behind where Raul was sitting. We all jumped in our seats as a large, matronly-looking woman with bright red hair and a billowing, flowered summer dress heaved into the room as if she'd broken the offensive line and was making for the quarterback.

"Yow! I am so sorry, folks," she huffed. "That damn door always does that and I don't never seem to learn. I am so sorry I'm late but we had a little incident on the rail.

Some little guy was grindin' a rail from the top of the stairs and did himself a little straddle ride, if you get the picture. He won't be singing baritone for a while, if you know what I mean."

She walked around the table, came directly over to me, and thrust out a meaty hand. "I'm Carolina Jones," she bellowed. "I own this place and glad to say so, liability insurance and all!"

I laughed and gladly took her hand in mine; I liked her immediately.

"I am so sorry to interrupt the festivities." I loved the way she apologized about everything—I could just hear her saying *I am so sorry for the terrible weather*, or *I am so sorry for the wart on your nostril*. "But, I have to steal Mr. Farber here for just a sec or two."

"You do?" I said. "Is there something wrong?"

"No, no! I am so sorry to have concerned you. It's nothing like that but," she clamped her hand around my elbow and leaned in close to my ear, "I do have to borrow you."

She all but yanked me to my feet and I bleated, "Be right back," to the folks as she hustled me out the door.

"Don't know if he'll be back today or not, actually," she called over her shoulder. "I am so sorry about this, folks." This time she didn't sound like she'd meant it.

"What's going on?" I pleaded as she ushered me toward the archway leading out to the ramps.

We stepped out onto the lot and she pointed to the top of the half-pipe. Just as I looked up I saw someone execute a perfect handplant, pausing for a brief moment with feet and board in the air before arching around, landing his board back on the ramp and skating back down into the U and up the other side. A helmet and pads hid the skater well, but I could still tell that he was no kid. Oddly, something about him looked familiar. I watched him repeat the same stunt over and over, perfecting the move a little more on each pass.

"I opened this place about three years ago," said Carolina. "I wanted our kids to have a safe place to skate. A place where they could help each other learn all the fine skills and characteristics that a great skater needs without worry about the, well, seedier elements of the streets. I watch out for them, try to keep them from hurting themselves too much, and fix them up when they do. Some of these kids have broken families, some are pretty well off, but when they're here, I'm the mama."

"Very cool," I said, watching the guy on the ramp. "But obviously it's not just kids that come here."

"No, it's not just kids." She put her fingers to her lips and whistled like a pro. "He's no kid, but he's an important part of the spirit of this place."

The skater looked our way and came to a stop by sliding on his knees to the bottom of the U. He kicked up his board, grabbed it in his hand, and set it down on the asphalt as he walked toward us. When he pulled off his helmet, I saw him clearly and realized with a start why he looked so familiar. He broke into a run, thumped into me with arms wide open, and clasped them around me in a great bear hug.

"Dude!" he shouted into my left ear. "It's awesome to see you! Really, really awesome!"

We pushed back from each other and I caught my breath. "Edg! Jeez, man, what are you doing here?"

He looked as fit and lively as the last time I'd seen him, two years earlier. His goatee showed a little more salt in the pepper, and his hair was cropped to Marine length, a good look for him. His requisite Hawaiian shirt was patterned with large, colorful blooms and his baggy, khaki pants billowed out from a waist even slimmer than I remembered.

"Had a little business to take care of, so I thought I'd come over to the mainland and do it in the flesh—give myself a chance to reconnect with some old buds."

"I just wanted to see the look on your face, Steve," laughed Carolina. "And it was worth it, I must say! I thought I was gonna have to practice my CPR on you. I'll leave you two to catch up.

I need to at least make an appearance at that meeting I'm supposed to be hosting." She waved and thundered back into the building.

Edg looked toward the parking lot. "You still have that Mustang of yours?"

"I sure do, Edg. She's still got a few miles on her."

"Well, then," he raised his eyebrows like the rascal that he was. "Let's blow this boneyard. We've got a lot to talk about, don't we?"

Yeah, we did, but that would have to wait. There was something I had to take care of first.

36.

Rich Delacroix greeted me in the ILGI reception area, and we walked back to his office in silence. He said something to his assistant, followed me into his office, and shut the door behind us. He perched himself on the edge of his large, slate desktop and I stood facing him with my hands in my pockets.

"I want you to know, Rich, that I really tried," I began without his asking me to. "I spent the day with Cam, even introduced him to some pretty sharp folks who all—out of the goodness of their hearts, mind you—were more than willing to share their knowledge with him. Just to help him out, you know?"

He nodded, so I pressed on.

"I don't want to say anything inappropriate, and I don't want to put this all on Cam, so let's just say that he and I just don't click. I have to admit that I was a little disappointed with myself, but, hey, it is what it is, and I'm clearly not the guy to work with him..."

The words ran out.

"I hope you understand, Rich."

"I do," he said simply.

"So, if I may ask, what happens with Cam now?"

"It's already happened," he said and pressed a button on his phone. "Ask her to come in now, please," he said into the speaker.

Spunky was the first word that popped into my brain when I saw her. She wore a navy dress suit and carried a black leather-covered notebook, which added to her sharp, professional mien.

"I'm Lisa Appleman," she said, not waiting for an introduction. We shook hands, and I must have cocked my head, or knitted my brow or done something to indicate that I didn't comprehend, because she quickly followed up with, "I'm the new SVP of sales."

Rich and I looked at each other. "That was fast," I said.

"Yeah, it was," said Rich. "But it didn't happen the way you think."

"Do you want to tell me about it?" I asked, hoping that he would.

"He wasn't fired," said Lisa in a compassionate voice that took me by surprise.

"And I didn't exactly demote him, either," added Rich.

"What do you mean, *exactly*?" I said. "Seems to me that you either did or you didn't."

"What I mean," Rich started to explain, "is that I didn't demote Cam."

Now I was really lost. "Well, who did, then?"

"Cam did."

I shook my head. "Not following you."

"Cam came in early this morning and said he'd been thinking

all night after spending the day, and apparently part of the evening, with you and your *friends*, he called them."

I did not want to rehash last night's discussion, so I kept quiet, for once.

"He said he realized that managing other people wasn't for him, at least for right now, and that he'd much rather just get back on the phones and sell. He was itching to break his own personal best sales records. He offered to relinquish his title immediately and asked if I'd let him keep his office so he could work without distraction and *burn it up*. So, what could I say? He gave us all the perfect solution, because—I'll be honest with you, Steve— that's exactly what I was going to offer him. Well, that or a severance package."

"Much better this way, though, isn't it?" I couldn't fight back a smile.

"Much," said Lisa. "He's on my team; I can't wait to see what he does. I'm going to do everything I can to support him."

Now, that's what I'm talkin' about, I thought. "Well, Lisa, if you ever need any help with him..." I began.

"Yes?"

"Well...I may want another crack at him, is all."

"Thanks," she said. "I'll remember that."

Yeah, I thought. *So will I.*

37.

I must have made a wrong turn as I walked down the hallway away from Rich's office. I thought reception would be on my right, but, instead, I was looking at a row of offices I'd never seen before. In an attempt to get my bearings I glanced around and *bam*! there he was in the office across the way.

Cam was working like a vortex: he had a phone on one ear and a headset wrapped around the other. An assistant was sitting in a chair next to his desk, sliding files in front of him as he talked into the mouthpiece in soft, rapid tones.

I tried to scoot on past without him seeing me, but he suddenly looked up and waved me in without missing a beat of rhythm on the phone. I heard him ask the person to hold, and he jabbed the button like a prizefighter.

"Farber," he said in a rush. "Sorry, you know, about last night. About the whole day. I know you think you wasted your time."

"Yeah, well, don't worry about it, Cam. I really do wish you great success; I hope you knock 'em dead." Okay, so it was a cliché.

"You didn't, though," he said as he took his call off hold.

"I didn't what?" I stage whispered, but as far as he was concerned, I was already gone. I gave a little wave, which he didn't see, and started to turn toward the door. That's when I saw it, lying open on the desk next to his stack of files.

Cam's Wake-Up Pad.

Déjà Vu

It was another one of those typical San Diego days: the sky was blue and bright, and the ocean was sparkling as it slapped its waves onto the shores of Mission Beach. I was sitting on the seawall, lost in thought and filled with a new sense of—what was it?—optimism, I guess.

It made my day, seeing that pad on Cam's desk. Something had stuck, and it was no small thing at that. I was actually impressed with his decision to give up management and go back on the phones. That took some kind of guts. Most people would have quit and gone in search of a new place, but he chose to stay and become a champion all over again, and this time he'd be doing what really trips his trigger. Come to think of it, I think Cam may just have found his frequency.

So I had to wonder, maybe Cam's world had changed a little, but did that qualify me as a change-the-world practitioner? I decided I wasn't ready to claim that, exactly, but it sure felt like progress. Best of all, after my exposure to the WUP, my conversations with Agnes, and the guidelines from the gathering at *SKATE!*, I felt that I had something tangible and helpful to bring back to the Jims on my next trip to Michigan.

I was jolted out of my musings by a sudden, sloppy lick on the side of my face. A jumbo-sized Golden Retriever had come up behind the seawall and ambushed me with a kiss.

"Sadie! How you doin', you big poochie?" I gave her a mighty scratch behind her ears.

Since Smitty had been house-sitting for Edg and taking care of Sadie for the last couple of years, I knew that the boys had to be close by. I spun around on the seawall, jumped down onto the boardwalk, and scanned the area.

I'd already realized that Edg's reappearance hadn't been as sudden as I'd thought. He'd been back in San Diego for a while without my knowing it.

His baby, XinoniX, the company he'd founded and retired from, was looking at an acquisition, and he'd come to town to help with the due diligence process. When Janice told him about my new coaching engagement, Edg started doing what he does best.

He helped me without my knowing it.

However, not at the expense of the fathomless joy he takes in messing with my head.

He wrote the note the same morning that Smitty had given it to me; he set up the lunch with Agnes and then came by the diner to spy on us. That's when he paid the tab. He got into my apartment, left his skateboard in my garage, and scribbled in my Wake-Up Pad just for fun. The guy delights in seeing me twist, squirm, lurch, writhe, and all the other words that you'll find in the thesaurus under struggle. In other words, he gets deep satisfaction in watching me try to come to terms with myself.

Do you have any idea how that makes me feel? Like the luckiest human being on the planet.

Getting Your Radical Edge

Set Up Your WUP

Choose a notebook or tablet—paper or electronic—to use as your first Wake-Up Pad and write these headings as a reminder of how to use it:

SCAN & EAVESDROP

Skim the bestseller lists, magazine racks, television listings, RSS and Twitter feeds, social media posts, and headlines of newspapers from around the country and the world. Scope out the room that you're sitting in and the crowd that you're walking with. Watch the trends in technology. Be an anthropologist. Study behavior. Notice things. Scan.

Listen to what people are saying at work, at home, in the supermarket, on the radio. What are your customers saying about their own challenges in their work? What are your neighbors saying about theirs? Did you hear something noteworthy? *Don't judge; record your observations in your WUP.*

PONDER

Periodically review what you've seen and heard. Now ask yourself: What do these things mean to me and mine? What are the implications for and the impact on my business, my life, the world? What other questions do I need to ask about what I've seen and heard?

Also ask: What's most important in my life? Why? What's my frequency? How do I consistently live in tune with it? What, if anything, is missing?

This is your space to consider anything—anything at all. *Don't edit, don't judge; just reflect, and let it roll in your WUP.*

TALKING POINTS

Recruit a team of fellow Extreme Leaders: your team at work, your fellow volunteers in your community efforts, your family, neighbors, and friends. Choose a time and place to gather, talk, kick it around, commiserate, and conspire; a time to compare notes on your experiences as human beings.

List the things you want to bring to the group's attention, the things you find interesting, funny, odd, inspiring; the things you need help understanding. The things you find noteworthy. *Note what you learn from your team in your WUP.*

TRY THIS

Now that you've scanned, eavesdropped, pondered for a while, and talked about it with some trusted kindred spirits, it's time to do something. Do something bold, something audacious. Something that could change the world for the better. Write your responses to the following prompts:

These are the things I'm going to experiment with...

These are the things I'll change right now...

*These are the commitments I make to the
people around me and to myself...*

These are the people I'll need to help get it all done...

Write all your ideas in your WUP.

Now that your WUP is primed and ready to go, keep it handy as you explore the following pages and use it to capture your thoughts, ideas and plans because you're going to have a lot to ponder, to talk about, to try.

You, my friend, are about to take a Radical Leap forward.

Stoke Your Business

*I may not have the capacity to love everyone,
but I do have the capacity to act as if I do and
run my business accordingly.* — Agnes Golden

*Do what you love in the service of people
who love what you do.* — Pops Maritime

Describe what you do at work, and then answer the following questions:

What do you love about it?

What don't you love?

What keeps you from loving it more?

TAKE A STORY INVENTORY

Think of the people you encounter at work as either internal or external to your business. Write down the names of one or two key internal people—colleagues, employees, staff, managers, partners, associates, et cetera. Write down the name(s) of one or two key external people—customers, vendors, suppliers, et cetera.

Now list everything you know about each person beyond the function he or she serves. Assess how much you know or don't know about each as a human being.

Ask each person to tell you one important story or event from his or her life. Look for an opportunity to find out more during your next conversation. Ask each to share with you his or her number one business challenge. Ask if there's some way you can be of service—something you can do to help with each person's challenge. Even if that person declines your offer, he or she will always appreciate your asking.

Now pick one to two more people and do it again. Repeat until you run out of people—for the rest of your life, in other words.

Amp Your Life

But it's not about finding your frequency by ruling out
everything else; on the contrary, it's about finding the frequency
that includes all those other important values and ideals.
The very act of trying to wrap it all together is what's really
important, because to do that you have to get very clear on
what you mean by each value and principle. You have to define,
think through, and understand each to its core, and evaluate
your life against each one. The clearer you get, the closer
you get to the frequency that pulsates through your life and
characterizes who you really are. — Agnes Golden

TUNE IN TO YOUR FREQUENCY.

List five values or principles that are most important to you in
the way you live your life. Write down your best definition of
each value. It only has to make sense to you.

Read through your list and your definitions. Now tune in to
one by considering the following perspectives. Which *one* of
these values—

is the most important to you in the way you live your life?

has the clearest meaning for you?

feels the best?

most accurately describes who you really are?

best describes how you'd like others to know you?

most fully encompasses your other values?

energizes you when you think about it?

if it were a radio station, would you turn it up the loudest?

That's your frequency.

AMP IT UP.

Think of all the roles you play in your life at work, at home, in the community, and with your family and friends. To what degree do you live by your frequency in each of those roles? In other words, at what volume does your frequency play in each role?

For the next week, take notes in your WUP about how your frequency shows up—or doesn't—in your activities in the roles you play. Then work on the solution(s) to this question:

What can you change about your activities, your attitude, your priorities, or your choices that will bring you more in tune with your frequency and reduce the static in your life?

If you're more of a visual person, you can use these frequency worksheets to help you focus your thinking:

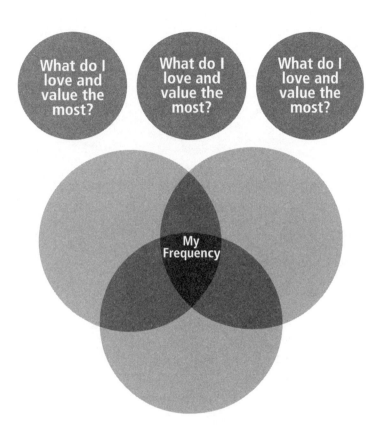

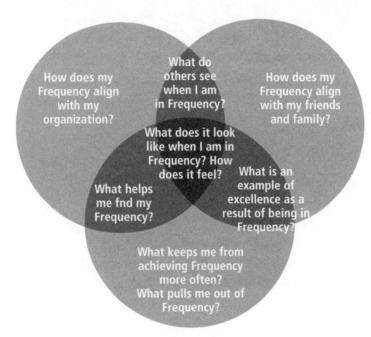

How does my Frequency align with my organization?

What do others see when I am in Frequency?

How does my Frequency align with my friends and family?

What does it look like when I am in Frequency? How does it feel?

What is an example of excellence as a result of being in Frequency?

What helps me fnd my Frequency?

What keeps me from achieving Frequency more often? What pulls me out of Frequency?

Change the World

Define what you mean by "world" and get clear on how you want that world to be different from the current reality. "World" doesn't have to mean the very fabric of human existence, although it certainly could be. It could be the world of your customers, neighborhood, industry—or the world of one person, for that matter. You define it for yourself.
— Ronald Perricone and *SKATE!*

FOUR *SKATE!* GUIDELINES FOR CHANGING THE WORLD

What is your world—the world you'd like to change?

Who is in it?

What is your relationship to these individuals?

Why do you care about them?

Why do you care so deeply about this world?

How do you want your world to be different than it is today?

Be specific about what changes need to happen and what a changed world will look like in the future.

Act as if your every action has a direct impact on the world. In other words, perform every deed as if it will either improve the world or damage it. — Ronald Perricone and *SKATE!*

List the first three steps you personally need to take in order to create the change you described.

    1.

    2.

    3.

Set a deadline for Step #1. If the above quote were literally true, what would you do differently starting right now?

Don't judge yourself based on the outcome of your efforts. If you succeed, don't take credit for it; if you fail, don't blame yourself. The only thing you take credit for is the fact that you tried. — Ronald Perricone and *SKATE!*

Write the above quote on a piece of paper and tape it to your bathroom mirror.

Now, review #2 and get going.

Never—never, ever—try to do it alone.
—Ronald Perricone and *SKATE!*

Build your own *SKATE!* Mastermind team and create your community for change.

Consider starting with one or two others and grow from there. Take your time finding like-minded people who want to change their worlds for the better and who fully believe that, with help, they can get it done. These are people you'd love to spend time with, people who are different from you, yet whose frequencies are harmonious with your own. Most importantly, build a team of people who can contribute to one another.

Experiment and find the best structure for your meetings. Whatever works for you will be the right way. Try this meeting process:

Take turns reading new entries from your WUPs.

Have an open, no holds barred conversation about your findings and observations.

Give a progress report on each person's change the world project and identify areas that need help, ideas, or solutions.

Brainstorm ideas and solutions, as a group, for each project.

Take a few minutes of solo time to record notes in your WUPs.

The Extreme Leadership Saga Continues!

Take your Extreme Leadership to the a deeper level with Steve Farber's *Wall Street Journal* and *USA Today*-bestseller, *Greater Than Yourself: The Ultimate Lesson of True Leadership*. Read on for a sample.

Greater Than Yourself

By Steve Farber

Prologue

The obsession seized me with all the subtlety of a sumo wrestler hopped up on anabolics.

I'd been playing guitar for thirty-five years, and I'd owned a couple of decent ones from time to time, but suddenly I needed—*needed*—that 1959 Gibson hollow-body electric hanging on the rack at Vintage Brothers Guitars in Carlsbad, California.

I don't know what it was. I'd seen nicer guitars, to be sure. There was nothing unusual about its sunburst finish, and with only one pickup in the middle position, the ES-330 wasn't considered the most desirable of collectable instruments. But other than a few minor nicks on the headstock, it was in perfect condition, and as I sat in the store's small demo room, playing it hour after hour, I fell deeper and deeper in love. The neck was fast, the tone, sweet, rich and mellow. Yeah, I was in love, man, but not all love and obsession winds up in marriage, so eventually I put it back on the rack, inquired just one more time about the price, and walked out into the salty, San Diego, Pacific Ocean air.

I've played better guitars, I kept telling myself, and I've seen better deals on vintage instruments. But as I walked toward my car, I couldn't shake it. Then the sumo got me, spun me around and shoved me back down the parking lot from where I'd come. My pace quickened as I approached the shop, and my wallet was out before I even got through the door. I paid the price and grabbed the case, and, minutes later, grinning a grin that tested the limits of my cheek-muscles, I tucked that baby into the passenger seat and buckled it in like the prize it was.

I had to have that guitar. *Had* to.

And now, just a few days later, I know why.

Chapter 1

I'm not really sure what to call it when things line themselves up without my slightest knowledge or influence. It's like someone is executing a profoundly interlaced conspiracy to make all the random pieces of my life fit together. What is it? Karma? Kismet? Synchronicity? I don't know, but it happens to me a lot, and more often than not it works out well. I just seem to meet the right teachers at the right time.

I've been blessed (maybe that's the word) with the opportunity to work with some of the world's preeminent thinkers in business leadership—like Tom Peters and Jim Kouzes to name a couple. And in recent years, under extremely odd and seemingly fortuitous circumstances, I've learned directly from some of the masters of Extreme Leadership—like William Maritime and Agnes Golden and Ted Garrison, names that'll be familiar to readers of my previous books.

I've done a pretty good job of conveying the lessons I've

learned along the way, and I think that's why I've made a bit of a name for myself in certain circles. Some have even used the words "Steve Farber" and "leadership guru" in the same sentence, which, although gratifying to my ego, makes me squirm like I have a load of wet worms in my socks.

Right teachers. Right time. Odd circumstances.

I was thinking I should print that on my business card, because it was starting to happen all over again.

I was back in my apartment on the bay side of the Mission Beach area of San Diego. The ocean and its frenetic boardwalk were a couple of blocks to the west, but calm, tranquil Mission Bay lay just a few short yards to the east of my building, affording a view through my living room window worthy of tourist's postcard.

I had returned from Carlsbad a couple hours earlier, cleared my agenda by taking care of a few time-bound tasks, and was now—finally!—ready to spend some quality time getting intimate with my new companion.

I gingerly placed the tattered, forty-nine-year-old, mottled brown guitar case on the dining room table, flipped open the latches, lifted the top, and let my gaze linger over the sunburst-colored curves of my new six-string babe.

Sitting on a barstool with the guitar propped in my lap, I twisted the tuning knobs until the sound was just right and fired off a couple of quick blues licks in the key of E. I'd plug it in later; for now I was enjoying the smooth feel of the Brazilian rosewood fingerboard and the muted, rich sound resonating off its un-amplified, maple body. I was just about to settle in for a few hours of serious playing (which sounds like an oxymoron—but it's not), when something in the case caught my eye. I set the guitar in a stand and got up to take a closer look.

The pink, plush lining on the inside bottom of the case was pulled slightly back at the seam and a small, yellowed piece of paper stuck out from under the fabric. I pinched the corner and pulled on it gently. It slid easily from under the velvet and revealed itself to be a handwritten note.

I felt a voyeuristic jolt similar to what an architect must feel when finding a relic that gives a glimpse into another's life in another time.

Dear Jessica,

This guitar is my gift to you. It was made in 1959, thirty-one years before I taught you your first lesson. What a player you've become in just five short years, and now that you're old enough to vote and on your way to school and the distractions of adult life, you'll need this guitar to remind you of your wonderful musical gift. And may it help you to become a better player than I ever hoped to be. I have no doubt you will.

You have brought this old teacher of yours more joy than you could possibly know and I want you to know that I'm very, very proud of you.

Your friend and teacher,
GZ

"You've been around, haven't you?" I said to the guitar in the stand.

I read the note one more time and tried to imagine the teacher, the student and the strong bond that had obviously existed between them. It was an unusual thing, that kind of connection. I'd been lucky enough to experience that student-teacher bond in my professional life, and I knew how rare and priceless a thing it could be, so, naturally, I found myself wondering where these people were today and what, if anything, had happened with Jessica's life as a guitarist—or if she even continued playing at all.

The way I figured it, (I had to use a calculator, I admit), this note was written somewhere around 1995, and if Jessica had just been reaching college age, that would put her in her early thirties today.

Had "GZ's" pride been well-placed? Had Jessica grown into the kind of adult he'd hoped she would? And why, if their relationship had been as special as the teacher's note implied, had Jessica eventually gone on to sell this wonderful and sentimental gift? And you'd think if she'd returned even a little of her teacher's affection, she'd at least have kept the note.

I know I would have.

Given my sudden and intense curiosity about all this, I found myself faced with two possible paths: I could either make up imaginary answers to these questions, or I could snoop around to see if I couldn't uncover the real story of Jessica and GZ.

And I bet you can guess which road I traveled by.

Chapter 2

Obviously, the name, Jessica, and the initials, GZ, weren't a whole hell of a lot to go on, so I did the only thing I could think of at the moment. Vintage guitars get bought, sold, and traded more often than the uninitiated might think, so it was, to say the least, unlikely that Jessica had just walked in to the guitar shop and sold it to them. Nevertheless, I had to give it a shot. I called, asked for the owner of the store, and begged him for the name of the person who'd sold them the guitar.

"Sorry," he said. "I really can't help you with that."

"I understand," I said, disappointed. "You have to protect the confidentiality of your customers."

He laughed. "Yeah, I guess I do, but that's not what I mean. I bought it at a local guitar show from another dealer, so I just don't see how you're going to be able to track down the previous owners. There's no telling how many times that guitar's changed hands."

I thanked him and was just about to hang up when he asked me to hold on for a second.

"I don't know if this'll help you," he said. "But there was a guy in here the other day asking about that same guitar. Said he had a friend that used to have one just like it, and that he may be interested. But he hasn't come back yet."

My heart did a little zippity-zip. I wondered if that ever happened to the *Law and Order* guys when they got a lead. "You wouldn't happen to know his name, would you?"

"Dude," he said. "What kind of a salesperson do you think I am? Of course I took his name. Hold on..."

He left me hanging for a minute while I listened to him rustle through some papers.

"Here it is: Charles Roland."

"That's great," I said, and spelled the name back to him.

"And I bet you want his number, too, don't you?"

"I love you," I said.

Chapter 3

I left a message on Charles Roland's voice mail. I told him briefly about the guitar and the note, and requested that if, by chance, he might know anything about any of this, that he please give me a call or drop me an email. I left all my contact info and, not expecting any kind of response, figured that would be the end of the line for my fleeting life as a private investigator.

So, with my fantasy tucked neatly away with my guitar and the note folded in my shirt pocket, I decided to take a scenic drive up the coast and enjoy the impending sunset. I got in my car, headed up through La Jolla and soon found myself entering the posh and charming little town of Del Mar. It had been a while since I'd stopped to fully take in the spectacle of the sun disappearing over the western horizon, so I decided to treat myself to a late-afternoon appetizer at Il Fornio and watch Mother Nature's show from atop the Del Mar plaza.

I parked the car in the lot and took the elevator to the open courtyard on the top floor, which afforded a spectacular, panoramic view of the blue water shining brilliantly in the light of the descending sun. I stepped up to the open-air bar at the restaurant, ordered calamari and a diet coke with lemon and found an open table pushed up against the glass wind barrier.

I took a quick moment to scan the email on my iPhone and saw that I had a recent message. My chest thumped when I read the subject line: "A response from Charles Roland." Polite and formal in his tone, Mr. Roland wrote that he was "surprised and delighted" to hear about that note and that, yes, he did know the people involved and would love to meet me so he could see it firsthand.

So, there it was. *Easy as pie*, I thought.

After a couple of terse, back-and-forth emails, we agreed to meet the next morning at Peet's Coffee in Pacific Beach, just a mile or so up Mission Blvd from where I lived.

So, the following morning found me at Peet's, sitting at an outside table and sipping a double shot mocha while I watched the early morning traffic. The ocean was just a block away and the salt smell was, thankfully, much stronger than that of the exhaust fumes. The marine layer fogged out the sunshine, and as the caffeine lifted the fog from my brain, I considered the meeting that was just about to take place. I was surprised at how flippin' excited I was to hear this story, to learn about Jessica and GZ. You'd almost think I didn't have any friends of my own.

"Good morning, Mr. Farber."

I looked up at, I assumed, Charles Roland.

"And you would be Charles Roland?" I said, rising politely from my chair.

"That I would," he said as we clasped hands.

Charles's appearance was unusual in that there wasn't anything unusual about his appearance. He was the kind of guy who'd easily blend in with forty-something, middle-class, suit-and-tie kind of crowd—not exactly the profile of the typical, San Diego beach collection, but I figured that he was on his way to the office and was dressed for that world, not this.

He wore his dark brown hair in a conservative cut that gave the impression that he visited his barber every couple of weeks. His white shirt was starched and crisp and pressed in a way that, no matter what I did or had done to them, my shirts would never conform to. He wore a simple, gold band on the ring finger of his left hand. I added to that his gray suit and dark, patterned tie and came out with one resounding conclusion: Charles Roland was some kind of a corporate stiff. An office drone in worsted wool.

Let me just say in my own defense that I am not a judgmental person. I am, quite likely, one of the most accepting people you'll ever meet, and I say that with utmost humility. In other words, my rush to judgment here was entirely out of character. Looking back on it now, I missed the more subtle signs about his true nature, which, in retrospect, should have been as obvious as a tuba.

I offered to get him a coffee and he declined.

"So, Charles," I started in cautiously. "This is such a strange little scenario. Kind of romantic, in a way, isn't it?"

"I suppose so," he said, almost mechanically. "May I see the note, please?"

I handed it to him and watched him read. Except for a very slight rising of the eyebrows, he looked quite emotionless.

He handed the note back to me and said nothing.

"So..." I just couldn't read this guy. "Jessica and GZ," I said into the awkward silence. "What can you tell me about them?"

"May I be blunt, Steve?" It must have been a rhetorical question, because he didn't wait for my answer. "I'm not so sure I want to do that."

That was the last thing I expected him to say. "What do you mean?" I said, shocked. "I thought that's why you came to meet me."

"I said I'm not sure, yet. I didn't say no."

I waited for him to continue.

"I checked you out last night, Steve. Looked through your website, read some of your stuff. I think I have a pretty good sense of what you're all about—professionally, anyway."

"Okay. Good. I guess. But what's my work got to do with this?"

"That's the thing. I think you'll find it's got everything to do with it—that is, if you are who your materials claim you to be."

"Okay," I said, annoyed now. "How long are you gonna do this cryptic thing? Am I going to get to meet these people or not? Or hear about them, at least?"

"My apologies, Mr. Farber, for being so vague. Here's the situation: for one thing, I'm very protective of the privacy of the individuals involved here—one of them, in particular, with whom I work. I'm sure you understand."

"Okay," I said. "Sounds reasonable."

"So, I don't want to waste their time with a...what...curiosity seeker. Any interaction with them needs to be...I guess I'd call it...meaningful for them."

"Meaningful," I repeated.

"Yes. And for another thing, there's a value in this for you, too, way beyond what you expected when you contacted me."

"Really," I said, more than a little skeptical now. "Like what?"

"Like what made their relationship so special in the first place. Something was put in place between them—an operating principle, you might call it—that has developed into a way of life that goes way beyond 'GZ,' as you keep calling him, and his young student. And given the kind of work you do, and the leadership lessons you claim to advocate and believe in—it would be well worth your while to understand the principle before you meet the people. And, in fact, I've been authorized to say that they have no interest in sharing their experience with you unless you get a grasp of this principle first. Are you interested, Steve?" Again, he didn't wait for my answer. "Because if you are, I'm willing to teach you about it. And if you're not..."

"Uh huh?" I asked, feeling pretty sure I knew what he was going to say.

"If not, we say goodbye right now. No harm; no foul."

He must have seen something in my face.

"Does that sound harsh?" he asked.

"A little," I said. "Not to mention a touch bizarre."

"Perhaps," he said. "But I assure you that's the way they want it. That's the deal; take it or leave it."

I almost got up and left. I swear I came that close to bagging this whole thing—I mean who did this Roland guy think he was? Who did he think I was, for that matter? I was busy too, you know. He assumed I had all this time on my hands—like I had nothing better to do with myself. And who was he to teach me? Like I couldn't teach him a thing or two.

But as I worked through my indignant inner gyrations and calmed down a little, I was left with one clear, undeniable feeling: my heart was sinking at the thought of this whole thing going up in a puff of my fragile ego.

"So," I said off-handedly. "What do you call this life-changing 'operating principle' of yours? And it better not be *The Secret*, or we're done right now."

He sat up straight and clapped his hands together in an unexpected burst of glee.

"Cool!" he shouted, morphing from a virtual cadaver to an animated extrovert right before my eyes. "Greater Than Yourself, we call it. Or GTY, for short."

As soon as I'd said yes, he'd transmogrified. The near-instantaneous shift in his personality—the new, comical energy in his voice, enlivened expression on his face, and enthusiastically gesticulating hands—really threw me. Apparently, my initial snap-judgment of Charles Roland, Company Zombie, had been way off.

"So, what happens now?" I managed to say

"I," he said, wiggling his brows like Groucho Marx, "am taking you to school."

He fished a legal pad and pen from his leather Tumi briefcase and set them on the table in front of him.

"And me without my knickers and paste," I said. "What kind of school?"

"GTY School," said Charles. "And here's the agenda."

He held up three fingers on his left hand and ticked them off one at a time with the index finger of his right. "First, I give you an overview of the three tenants of GTY; second, we take a field trip to visit a practitioner and veritable guru on the subject; and, third, you do homework."

"Homework? Seriously?" I was never much of a fan.

"Yes. Tonight. Homework. Is there a problem?"

"*American Idol*'s on."

He ignored me. "And then if you pass the final and demonstrate worthiness by walking over hot coals, I'll take you to meet them."

"Hot coals? Seriously?" It sounded far-fetched, but, after all, Tony Robbins did live around here.

"Only if you want," he grinned.

The whole thing sounded overly dramatic and more than a little contrived, but Charles seemed so eager to get on with it that I just held my breath and jumped in.

"I'll take a pass on the blisters, but sign me up for the rest, I guess."

"A fine choice," he said, tearing off the wrinkled top page of the pad. "Shows excellent intellectual discrimination."

"Do you actually get paid for this, Charles?"

"I am indeed on the payroll, pal," he said. He wrote *Greater Than Yourself* across the top of a clean, fresh page and turned the pad around to face me. "So, how about you cut the smartass shtick and help me earn my keep?"

There's nothing like starting out your first day of school with a good, hard spanking from the teacher.

Raising someone up does not reduce your stature—in fact,
it exalts you in ways you have to experience to believe.
Greater Than Yourself shows how you can begin improving the
world by giving of yourself. It's a wonderful message wrapped in
a highly entertaining, well-written story.
— Ken Blanchard, coauthor of *The One Minute Manager*®
and *Leading at a Higher Level*

Greater Than Yourself: The Ultimate Lesson of True Leadership is available from Crown Business.

About the Author

Steve Farber is the Founder and CEO of The Extreme Leadership Institute, an organization devoted to helping its clients in the business community, non-profits, and education to create award-winning cultures and achieve radical results.

Former vice president and official mouthpiece—that's what it said on his business card—of legendary management guru, Tom Peters Company, Farber is a seasoned leadership coach and consultant who has worked with a vast array of public and private organizations in virtually every arena, from the tech sector to financial services, manufacturing, healthcare, hospitality, entertainment, retail, public education, nonprofits, and government.

He's the author of *Greater Than Yourself: The Ultimate Lesson of True Leadership*, which debuted as a *USA Today* and *Wall Street Journal* bestseller; *The Radical Leap: A Personal Lesson in Extreme Leadership*, which was named as one of the 100 Best Business Books of All Time; *The Radical Edge*, which was hailed as "a playbook for harnessing the power of the human spirit"; and *Love Is Just Damn Good Business*, published by McGraw-Hill in September of 2019.

He lives, as you may have guessed, in San Diego.

WORK WITH STEVE FARBER AND THE EXTREME LEADERSHIP INSTITUTE TEAM

Listed as one of Inc's global Top 50 Leadership and Management Experts, Steve Farber is a leadership pioneer, strategist, keynote speaker and bestselling author on Extreme Leadership. His expertise is in creating organizational cultures where leadership is not just an opportunity and obligation for those in authority, but for everyone at all levels.

His accessible, deeply inspirational, and eminently practical Radical LEAP framework is widely used across the business, non-profit and education spectrum. Farber has been credited with redefining leadership in deeply personal yet practical terms and re-energizing thousands of people to make a significant difference in their businesses, personal lives, and the world around them.

Farber's Extreme Leadership Institute team develops their programs with one thing in mind: radical results for their clients. As a result, they have helped more than 20 companies achieve "Best Place to Work" status.

Steve and The Extreme Leadership Institute team can work with you by:

- Delivering practical, inspiring and entertaining keynote speeches
- Operationalizing LEAP in your business to earn a competitive advantage
- Embedding the practices of Extreme Leadership in your organization's DNA
- Providing significant on-going leadership learning and development

- Creating and amplifying deep employee engagement
- Developing your award-winning culture
- Helping you to achieve radical results

Steve has worked with or spoken to hundreds of organizations large and small in virtually every industry--from the tech sector to financial services, manufacturing, health care, hospitality, entertainment, public education, retail, and government. His clients include such notable organizations as American Greetings, Intel, TriNet, Hyatt, Ernst & Young, Qorvo, and BNI.

To book Steve Farber for your next event visit
www.SteveFarber.com

To learn about The Extreme Leadership Institute's full offering of consulting, coaching, and training services, visit
www.ExtremeLeadership.com

Take the LEAP assessment online and receive lots of great resources too at **www.LeapAssessment.com**

BRING THE EXTREME LEADERSHIP WORKSHOP TO YOUR ORGANIZATION

Develop Extreme Leaders throughout your company or team with The Extreme Leadership Workshop. This highly adaptable workshop is designed as a one-day (8-hour) workshop but can be tailored to 4 hours or extended to 2 full days, depending on your specific needs. It is facilitator-led and includes individual reflection and action-planning, small group interaction, and built-in videos featuring author, Steve Farber, explaining and applying the Extreme Leadership concepts. It also includes a series of exclusive, follow-up videos from Steve to keep your participants on the path to Extreme Leadership.

Become Certified to Teach The Extreme Leadership Workshop. There are only a handful of certified, licensed, Extreme Leadership Workshop facilitators on the planet, and you now have an opportunity to be one of them. In this powerful and transformational workshop, you'll explore the key tenets of the Extreme Leadership Framework—Cultivating Love, Generating Energy, Inspiring Audacity, and Providing Proof—and learn how to apply them to your personal and professional leadership challenges. And then, with personal coaching from Steve Farber and his team, you'll be given all the tools, resources, and experience you'll need to facilitate this workshop for others.

At the end of the program, you'll be licensed to offer this unique workshop to your clients, your company, your team, your colleagues, or your community; just as important, you'll become part of our exclusive facilitator "tribe." For more information email **info@ExtremeLeadership.com** or call us at **858-513-4184.**

CONNECT WITH STEVE FARBER!

facebook.com/stevefarber

/stevefarber

@stevefarber

@Steve Farber